WHO'S FOR
THE GAME?

WHO'S FOR THE GAME?

The story of the men from four Birmingham
sports clubs who died in World War I

DOUGLAS H. SMITH MBE

BREWIN BOOKS

BREWIN BOOKS
56 Alcester Road,
Studley,
Warwickshire,
B80 7LG
www.brewinbooks.com

Published by Brewin Books 2019

A CIP catalogue record for this book is available
from the British Library.

ISBN: 978-1-85858-557-4

Printed and bound in Great Britain
by Bell & Bain Ltd.

Contents

Acknowledgements

This book has its origins in a talk I gave at Moseley Ashfield Cricket Club in 2014 to commemorate the players from the four clubs who died in the First World War. To research it I had to look at the names on the three memorials. This in itself was a problem because of the number of names but also because in some cases the details on the names was too brief and in some cases completely wrong. I have used my best endeavours to ensure that the book is as accurate as possible and hopefully my educated guess are the truth for each man.

The sources used are mainly available on the internet. The obvious one is the wonderful Commonwealth War Graves Commission site (*www.cwgc.org*). By searching through the various sites on the internet I was able to track individual names and the battalions they were in. The most useful sites for these were Forces War Records (*www.forces-war-records.co.uk*), the Wartime Memories Project (*www.wartimesmemoriesproject.com*) and the Long, Long Trail (*www.longlongtrail.co.uk*). The microfilmed local papers at the Library of Birmingham (*www.Birmingham.gov.uk/centrallibrary*) has excellent details of individual soldiers. For one name I was fortunate to have a copy of 'Lance's War' by Jane Stanley which explains in detail what happened to Hugh Lancelot Evers. When I gave the initial talk Edwina Rees was in the audience. Since then she and her colleagues have taken the research on men from Moseley to a whole new level with superb background detail on the men on their local memorials (*www.moseley-society-org.uk*).

As always my thanks goes to my big brother David R. Smith who has put up with me continually asking him for help and then trawling through *www.ancestry.co.uk* to answer my questions. Finally, as with anything I do, my very grateful thanks goes to my wife, Janice, who puts up with me sitting with the laptop on my lap whilst watching the TV, or in bed first thing in the morning, or when we are just about to go out and I'm still working, or last thing at night before the lights go out.

Introduction

Who's for the game?

"Who's for the game, the biggest that's played,
The red crashing game of a fight?
Who'll grip and tackle the job unafraid?
And who thinks he'd rather sit tight?
Who'll toe the line for the signal to 'Go!'?
Who'll give his country a hand?
Who wants a turn to himself in the show?
And who wants a seat in the stand?
Who knows it won't be a picnic – not much –
Yet eagerly shoulders a gun?
Who would much rather come back with a crutch
Than lie low and be out of the fun?
Come along, lads –
But you'll come on all right –
For there's only one course to pursue,
Your country is up to her neck in a fight,
And she's looking and calling for you."

Jessie Pope 1914

There's a field in a suburb of Birmingham, surrounded by 1960s houses, where cricket is played. It has been played here since 1900. Its pavilion was built in April 1914 and the cricket team's men went to war in August 1914. 18 of them did not return nor did 12 of the men who played for the football team they started. Their deaths are recorded on a wooden memorial plaque in the entrance hall. Twenty yards to the right of the front door, until October 2018, was a stone memorial to one of the most famous rugby clubs in the country with a further 18 names. The land is owned by one of the oldest golf clubs in the city and its clubhouse has another wooden memorial with a further four names.

This is the unique story of four famous sports clubs in Birmingham and the members of those clubs who perished in the First World War: Ashfield Cricket Club, Moor Green Football Club, Moseley Rugby Club and Moseley Golf Club.

I cannot tell why they went to war and can only speculate. Jessie Pope's poem is full of jingoism, of doing the right thing and of doing one's best. Perhaps many of them were caught up with the jingoism but also I would like to think that there was more to it than this and that they did it because their friends and teammates were doing it and they didn't want to let them, or their families down. They believed that they were doing the right thing in the prevailing attitude of the time. Yes they did it because they saw it as their duty but not blindly. I am sure that death and injury were in their minds and many would have gladly accepted coming home on a crutch. They did it unselfishly thinking of the greater good and I mourn their loss. I mourn for the hearts that were broken when they didn't return. I mourn for the good they would have done in the world and tears come to my eyes when I stand, with head bowed, thinking of their passing.

This is their story, not mine. Their lives were wasted by war and the years have passed but their stories will not be forgotten.

WE WILL REMEMBER THEM

Chapter 1

The Four Clubs

In the second half of the 19th century important social changes took place in Britain as the Industrial Revolution entered its final phase. From the 1840s the development of the railways had seen a transformation in the country as travel was revolutionised, time became standardised and communication greatly improved with newspapers, telegraph communication and an improvement in literacy. The growing middle class demanded education for their children on a level with those of the upper classes. Grammar Schools were established near to railway lines and they adopted the ethos of the Public Schools with their emphasis on sport and team spirit. The second half of the 19th century also saw the development of organised sport with rugby and football. Added to this was the growth of suburbia and the creation of golf clubs, including municipal golf clubs.

For the working classes there was less opportunity. In the early 19th century everyone had just Sunday off. By 1850, the average working week was 10 hours a day for six days. Then in 1871 the Bank Holiday Act gave workers a few paid holidays each year. Also in the 1870s some clerks and skilled workers began to have a week's paid annual holiday. However even at the end of the 19th century most people had no paid holidays except bank holidays. In the 1870s some skilled workers began to have Saturday afternoon off. In the 1890s most workers gained a half day holiday on Saturday and the weekend was born and with it weekend sport.

Moseley Rugby Club

Moseley Rugby Club was the oldest of the four clubs being founded in October 1873 as Havelock Football Club, an offshoot of Havelock Cricket Club whose members were looking for something to do in the wintery months. At the time rugby was a twenty a side game and they had just enough members to form a team. In 1874 the club was renamed Moseley Football Club and the famous red and black colours were used for the first time with matches being played in Balsall Heath and with the club's first captain being S.H. Deakin who led the side for the first four seasons. The club moved to various grounds across Balsall Heath and Moseley.

Over the next few years the Club became one of the strongest rugby clubs in the country winning the inaugural Midland Counties Challenge Cup defeating Leamington Rovers in the final. In 1883 the club played its first game at The Reddings, defeating Leicester and won the Midland Counties Challenge Cup for a second time when Coventry were beaten in the final. They won the cup again in 1884-85, 1885-86, 1886-87 all these under the captaincy of Albert Smith. In the 1888-89 season Moseley became the first team to defeat the first-ever international tourists to the British Isles, the New Zealand Natives or Maoris and yet again they won the Midland Counties Challenge Cup. In the 1889-90 John Rogers, who succeeded Albert Smith as captain, became Moseley's first international player, representing England against Wales. In 1890-91 Richard Cattell was one of three Moseley players who were elected original members of the Barbarians. In 1893-94 J. Fred Byrne won three England caps at full back and was described in 1898 as 'probably the best full-back that has ever represented England.' Under his captaincy, during the 1894-95 season, Moseley lost just one match out of 24 and went on to win the Midland Counties Challenge Cup again. They won it again in 1896-97. In 1899 Guy Evers, the brother of Hugh Lancelot Evers, toured Australia with the British Isles side and played in three of the four international matches.

In the 1900 Olympic Games held in Paris, Moseley had the honour of representing Great Britain losing to France in their only game, however, the team still finished third. In the new century Moseley continued to have internationals. In 1904-05 John Chamberlain made two appearances for the Barbarians, in 1905-06 Cecil Shaw won the first of his six England caps and John Cooper won his only caps in 1908-09.

The last season before the war saw Moseley again for the 19th time in the Midlands Counties Challenge Cup Final with their opponents being Coventry. The match played at Leicester saw Coventry win 13-0 but the result was challenged by Moseley because Coventry had fielded 2 players, Maddocks and Judge not on their list of players and were not living in the area. They had made the protest before the competition but Coventry declared that Moseley's action was 'unsportsmanlike' because their query was only a technical one. They admitted that the omission of Maddocks's name was accidental but stated that Judge had lived in the city for at least 10 years. Coventry then gave back the Cup because they were fed up with the wrangling. Then there were rumours that Moseley had also made technical infringements. The secretary of the club, J.N.R. Stafford made a robust defence of the club saying that though submitted their list of players late the Midland Counties Football Union had accepted

STIRRING SCENES IN RUGBY MATCH AT MOSELEY.

There was great interest taken in the semi-final of the Midland Counties Senior Cup played at Moseley on Saturday between Moseley and Belgrave Premier Works. The home team won, the scores reading: Moseley 10pts., Leicester Premier nil. (1) Leicester hard pressed. (2) A stormy scene in mid-field.

Semi-final of Midlands Senior Cup. Moseley 10 pts versus Leicester Premier Works 0 pts.

the list. The executive of the Union considered the matter and concluded that both clubs were at fault and decided that the Midland Counties Challenge Cup for 1913/14 should be declared null and void and that the cup should not be awarded to any club. Of the team who faced Coventry W.J. Pearce and E.C. Hill were killed in the war.

When the war began so many rugby players enlisted that on 4th September 1914 the Rugby Football Union asked all clubs to suspend their fixtures for the duration of the war. On 7th September Moseley announced that the club had decided to play no fixtures during the 1914/15 season and that The Reddings was to be offered for use by the military. By this stage 20 Moseley players had volunteered for active service. This offer was accepted and Moseley Football Club effectively closed down for the duration of the war and re-opened in September 1919.

Moseley Golf Club

Moseley Golf Club is the oldest golf club in Birmingham. It was founded in September 1892 on rented land from Mr Lane of Billesley Hall Farm and fields belonging to a Mr Parker. The original course consisted of 9 holes. The grass was much longer than modern courses and there were hazards such as

Billesley Farm in the 19th century.

streams, ditches, hedges and fences. The original entrance to the course was on the corner of Billesley Lane and Southlands Road. In 1900 Mr Lane gave up the tenancy of the farm and Moseley Golf Club took over the lease which included the farm house. In 1905 the Worcestershire Union of Golf Clubs was formed with Moseley as one of the founder members. In 1907 they acquired more land from Coldbath Farm and were able to extend the course to 18 holes. The new course was opened in 1908. In 1911 the incorporation of Yardley into Birmingham meant that the club was technically in Warwickshire but chose to remain in the Worcestershire Union.

Moseley Ashfield

Moseley Ashfield were founded in 1900 by a group of friends who enjoyed playing cricket with each other on open ground in Ashfield Avenue, Kings Heath. The friends challenged the newly formed Kings Heath Baptist Cricket Club to a match and on 23rd June 1900. The match was played at The Reddings and though Harry Caink scored 64 of the Friends' score of over 70 they eventually lost by a small amount. Just over a week after that first match, on 2nd July, a meeting was held at Walter B. Bach's house, Beverley, Ashfield Avenue, Kings Heath. The decision of the meeting was to form a cricket club and, as a compliment to Mr Bach, the club was called the Ashfield Cricket Club. A ground was rented from a local farmer, Mr Hincks, in Brook Lane, Billesley, for an annual rent of £1 10 shillings a year. The first captain of the team was Harry Caink who was then replaced by Leslie O. Butler who remained captain until the start of the war. Other noticeable officials with connections to the war memorial are: Claude Johnson who was vice-captain from 1911-1914 and then captain from 1919-1920; Maurice Hobson who was vice-captain of the 2nd XI in 1907, 1909 and 1910; Edward O'Brian who was secretary from 1902 to 1910, T. Alan Furse who was treasurer from 1919 to 1928; and Howard Hill who was match secretary from 1922 to 1931.

In 1901 the club moved to a ground in Stoney Lane and bought a caravan which they called 'The Bathing Machine' and used as a pavilion until 1906. They moved to their present ground in Yardley Wood Road then part of Coldbath Farm in 1906. At the same time they purchased a small pavilion from Bournville Linden Tennis Club for £10. It was formally opened by Walter Bach on 9th June 1906.

In May 1913 the 14th Annual General Meeting was held at Walter Bach's house. The Treasurer, Ted Basnett reported that there was a 1s 4d deficit in

The opening of the new pavilion on 9th May 1914.

the accounts for the previous season but that the dance in November had raised £15. The Captain, Leslie Butler, gave a summary of the 1st XI and 2nd XI performances for the previous season. The 1st XI had played 21 matches of which 8 were won, 8 lost and 5 drawn. He said that in the batting 'Dr C. Johnson proved himself the mainstay of the team and the good form showed by Messrs Arthur Baker and Howard Hill were worthy of mention.' He also thanked Claude Johnson for ably stepping in as Captain due to his Territorial duties. He said that the bowling was the weak part of the team due in part to the soft wickets caused by the unusually wet season but that Ted Basnett had been the only consistent performer. In the 2nd XI Harry Rawlinson topped the batting averages.

In November 1913 a special meeting was held at Mr Bach's house. This time the discussion centred on proposed ground improvements. These included the building of a new pavilion, enlarging the ground and playing space, and other minor improvements. The estimated cost was over £300 which was a not inconsiderable sum in those days but the members and friends met their target. On 9th May 1914 the new pavilion, with 1914 in lead in the glass on the front door, was opened by Mrs Bach. A large crowd assembled to mark the occasion.

Of those listed as contributing to the cost of the improvements the following did not make it home after the war: W. Furse, H.R. Rawlinson, F. Fawcett, M.

Hobson, E.J.C. Price, H. Ryan Bell, J. Balkwill and H.E. Foizey. Added to this were S. Halsey and C. Johnson who died after the War.

Moor Green Football Club

Moor Green Football Club was formed in 1901 by members of Ashfield Cricket Club who so enjoyed the comradeship of playing cricket that they wanted to continue it in the winter months. They didn't play 'competitive' matches until after the war. A large number of players from Ashfield also played for Moor Green although some played exclusively for Moor Green. Walter Bach was also the president of the football club. The records of the club were destroyed in 2005 in a fire at their beloved Moorlands but a few survive. At the 12th Annual Meeting of the Club at Walter Bach's home it is interesting to see that the Treasurer's report includes a sum of £5 18s 3d was owed to Ashfield Cricket Club. Of those present the following were killed in the war: Johnson, Rawlinson, Price, Hobson, O'Brien, Blackham, Furse and Halsall. In the 1911/12 season of the 27 games played 12 were won, 9 lost and 6 drawn. The club fielded three teams.

In 1913 the records are incomplete but they won 10 out of 28. At the end of the 1913 season such was the influx of new members that plans were made to acquire an extra ground adjacent to their present ground and previously rented by Camp Hill Old Edwardians. A change of kit colour was also suggested for the club with white shorts being replaced by dark blue but this was defeated, however, there was a change of sock colour to alternate light and dark blue rings. There were no records for the 1913/1914 season as the annual meeting would have been held in September 1914 and by then its players were at war.

Chapter 2

1914

On 28th June 1914 the heir to the Austro-Hungarian throne and his wife were assassinated by a Serbian nationalist in Sarajevo. The repercussions of those deaths were profound leading as they did to a world war in which millions were to die. At first the gravity of the situation wasn't obvious. It took nearly a month for the Austrians to respond. On 23rd July they sent an ultimatum to the Serbians with a list of what they wanted them to do. On 24th July the *Birmingham Daily Mail* reported the demands under the heading of 'New War Danger' and went on to say that Germany and France were both trying to localise the conflict. The Serbians agreed to all the Austrian demands apart from the one which would have allowed Austro-Hungarian officials onto Serbian soil to collaborate on the investigation into the murders. As a result, on 28th July, the Austrians declared war on Serbia beginning the bombardment of Belgrade on the next day. The Russians then began to mobilise on their border with Austria but because of their archaic war plans and railway system, ordered general mobilisation which meant mobilising on the German border. At 7pm on 31st July Germany had requested that France state whether it would remain neutral in a Russian-German war and demanded a response by 1pm on Saturday 1st August. At midnight on 31st July they had given Russia an ultimatum to demobilise within 12 hours. Ever since the Franco-Russian alliance of 1892, the Germans were afraid of a war on two fronts, against France and Russia at the same time and therefore had developed the Schlieffen Plan which involved attacking France through Belgium first, defeating them and then turning their attention to defeating the Russians.

The *Birmingham Daily Mail* of Saturday 1st August reported the events under the heading of 'England's Responsibility':

"While we are all still hoping against hope, it can hardly be denied that hour by hour the European situation grows darker. Yesterday was a day of ominous news: the proclamation of martial law throughout Germany, the complete mobilisation of the Russian army, the precautionary mobilisation in Holland and Belgium, and last but by no means least in significance the closing of our Stock Exchange and the phenomenal rise in the Bank rate from 4 to 8 percent."

It went on to mention the German ultimatum to Russia and then the threat to Belgium. It continued:

"... We cannot afford to see our friends in Europe crushed by a power which may afterwards fling the might of its overwhelming armies upon us; we cannot afford to see the integrity of Belgium and Holland destroyed and the coasts which from our own within a few hours journey held by an essentially hostile Power; we cannot afford to allow one nation on congeries of nations to have such dominance over Europe that our own existence is threatened or that we have to turn all our men into soldiers and our country into an armed camp."

The Russians had not made a response to the German ultimatum. In Britain it was the start of the Bank holiday weekend but Sir Edward Grey, the British foreign secretary, was frantically sending messages to other capital cities. On 28th July the First Lord of the Admiralty, Sir Winston Churchill, had begun the preliminary mobilisation of the Navy and now argued for full mobilisation. At 5pm on 1st August the Kaiser ordered mobilisation and then declared war on Russia and as a result their forces began to cross over into Luxemburg. By a secret agreement with the French Britain had pledged to use its Navy to protect the French coast from attack by the Germans and on that Sunday night the Admiralty called out the Fleet Reserve and Sir Edward Grey made it clear in the Commons that, whilst still pursuing a course for peace, the British Fleet would render all protection possible to the North and west coast of France if a German fleet came down the Channel or through the North Sea.

On the evening of 1st August the Belgium government received a letter from General Helmuth von Moltke, Chief of the German General Staff, saying that he had received news that the French were planning to invade Germany through Belgium and that in order to defend herself, Germany would need to enter Belgian territory as an act of self-preservation to 'anticipate this hostile attack'. Belgium was given 12 hours to come to allow the German onto their territory and if not the Germans would invade, 7am on Monday 3rd August. When that hour came the Belgium government defiantly rejected the German ultimatum. On the afternoon Sir Edward Grey addressed the Commons. He explained Britain's commitment to France through the 1904 Entente Cordiale and that he had given the French Ambassador the assurance that the Royal Navy would protect the French coast from naval attack by the Germans. He explained, too, that Britain had asked both France and Germany whether they would respect Belgian neutrality, in accordance with the Treaty of London of 1839; France had said yes, Germany had declined to answer. He went on to say Britain would suffer in the war whether they stayed in or out but that staying out, running away from the obligations of the Belgian Treaty, would harm Britain's honour, respect and interests in the rest of the World.

At 6pm, after alleging that the French had crossed into German territory and had also violated Belgian neutrality, Germany declared war on France. At 7.30pm the British Cabinet met again and agreed that Germany must withdraw its ultimatum to Belgium even though this would result in war if they did not. In the early hours of the morning of 4th August German troops crossed into Belgium territory and then, at 11pm, Britain declared war on Germany and mobilised its armed forces, its small standing army, the army reserves and the territorials.

1. ? Private George Pearce – 12252 3rd Battalion Worcestershire Regiment. And so the names from the memorials start with a possibility rather than a certainty. He appears on the Moseley Rugby Club Memorial. He was the son of the late James Pearce and of Hannah Pearce, of 200, Linden Road, Kings Norton, Birmingham. He died aged 29 on *23rd August 1914* and is remembered on the La Ferte-Sous-Jouarre Memorial. (*Moseley Rugby Club*). There are 2 other possibilities but neither has a Birmingham connection.

The 3rd Battalion Worcestershire Regiment were at Tidworth on the evening of the 4th August 1914 when the order for mobilisation was received. They worked hard to get the Battalion up to full strength and properly equipped and it was the second week in August before mobilisation was completed. Then for some days the 3rd Battalion stood fast awaiting orders which didn't arrive until the 12th August 1914. Early on the morning of the 13th August, about 5am, the 3rd Battalion left Tidworth for Southampton and sailed for France on S.S. Bosnian on the morning of 14th August landing at Le Havre. In hot weather and with cheering crowds they eventually arrived at Rouen before moving on to

Aulnoye and then marching to Marbaix. From 20th August their movements typify the movements of the BEF in those early days as they marched to and from various places before arriving at their billets in Ciply in the early hours of the morning of Sunday 23rd August. There they waited all morning and were about to eat their dinners when sudden orders came to advance. As they moved off the first shell shrieked overhead and burst behind them. They advanced towards Mons with the British Expeditionary Force (BEF).

The German armies had been advancing westwards through Belgium and had forced the Belgian army to withdraw northwards to the fortifications of Antwerp. The BEF took up a defensive position along the line of the Mons-Condé canal unaware of the strength of the forces coming to attack them. German cavalry had come in contact with the British outposts on August 22nd. To the right of the BEF the French Fifth Army at Charleroi was already sustaining the attacks of the German forces. The 3rd Battalion entrenched during the afternoon southwest of Ciply Railway Station but it was dusk before they finished. This was the second line of the defences held by the 3rd Division. There was gunfire on every side and shells burst amongst the slag heaps and there were fires in all directions. Crowds of terrified inhabitants came past on every road and track.

As darkness came the British front line withdrew and moved through the second line of defence. It was obvious that the fighting had been fierce as large numbers of wounded were with these forces. The 3rd Battalion came under attack in the early hours of the morning of 24th August forcing them to withdraw with 2 killed, 8 wounded and 11 missing.

2nd Lieutenant Geoffrey Vincent Pearce – 2nd Battalion Royal Warwickshire Regiment. He was the son of Sir William Pearce, M.P., and Lady Pearce, of Shepway Lodge, Walmer, Kent. He died aged 25 on *18th or 19th December 1914*.

Another possibility for G. Pearce. He fits the socio-economic profile for *Moseley Rugby Club* but I can't find a definite connection. On 18th December the 2nd Battalion Royal Warwickshire Regiment were ordered to capture the German position at Bois Grenier before Le Maisnil. As they emerged from their trenches they were met with ferocious rifle and machine gun fire but the casualties were so heavy that the survivors were forced to retreat to their own trenches. The Battalion lost its commanding officer, Lieutenant-Colonel Brewis, as well as eight other officers with another two wounded and one missing. The total casualties of other ranks were nearly 300.

Chapter 3

1915

By the start of 1915 the war on the Western Front had descended into the trench warfare stretching from the Channel to the Swizz border.

2. Lieutenant Vernon James Austin (On the *Moseley Rugby Club* Memorial he is listed as V.T. Austin) – 22nd Battery 34th Brigade Royal Field Artillery. He was the only son of Herbert Austin of Lickey Grange. He was born in Birmingham on the 21st November 1893, the only son of Sir Herbert Austin MP KBE and Helen (née Dron) of Lickey Grange, Bromsgrove in Worcestershire. He was educated as a boarder at St Cuthbert's, Malvern Link, and at the King's School Canterbury from September 1907 to July 1909, where he was a Probationary Scholar in Mr Bell's House and served in the Officer Training Corps.

Although destined to take over the family business Austin Motor Works from his father he was set on a military career and on the 6th January 1912 he was commissioned in the Special Reserve of the Royal Artillery as a 2nd Lieutenant. As an experienced motor car racer he was due to sail for Russia to take part in a race organised by the Automobile Club of Russia when war was declared in August 1914. He was promoted to Lieutenant, underwent further training at Bulford Camp on Salisbury Plain and sailed with the 22nd Battery 34th Brigade Royal Field Artillery in support of 2nd Infantry Division landing in France on the 17th August 1914. He saw action at the Marne, the Aisne and at Ypres. On the morning of the *26th January 1915* he and his commanding officer Lieutenant Colonel Sandilands went forward alone to reconnoitre near La Bassee. Whilst returning along an open stretch of road he was shot in the right side of his chest by a sniper. He lapsed into unconsciousness and died in a few minutes.

Sandilands wrote to his parents: "Your son, who was a Subaltern in my battery, was killed in action this morning about 11.30am. The poor boy and I were alone when he was shot by a sniper. He had accompanied me to a forward position in order to learn the ground, never at any time a very safe business but necessary. Coming back we had to pass an exposed piece of road. It was at this point that he was shot through the right breast by a rifle bullet, and died within a few minutes without regaining consciousness....I need hardly tell you what a gloom it has cast over officers and men of my battery, as everyone was so fond of him. He was such a cheery little chap and always showed such a stout front under fire. He was keen and capable officer and he is a great loss to the Brigade with all of whom he was so popular."

His body was brought back to England on the 6th February and after lying in the Chapel of the Innocents in Canterbury Cathedral, he was buried with full military honours in St Martin's Church, Canterbury on the 8th February in a service taken by the Headmaster, Reverend Dr McDowall. Cadets from the school played the Last Post and fired three volleys over the grave. Wreaths were laid on behalf of the King's School masters, the boys and the Officer Training Corps. Inside the church there is a plaque presented by the employees of the Austin Motor Company which reads "This tablet was erected in memory of a brave soldier by the employees of the Austin Motor Company of Birmingham, London and Manchester." His original grave marker is in the King's School Memorial Chapel, and he is commemorated at *Moseley Rugby Club*.

3. 2nd Lieutenant Gilbert Rowland Venables, 3rd Battalion King's Shropshire Light Infantry. He was the eldest son of Rowland George and Gertrude Venables, of Oakhurst, Oswestry, Shropshire. He was a barrister on the Oxford circuit and took a keen interest in the Poor Law being a member of the Oswestry Board of Guardians. He was an all-round sportsman and was captain of Oswestry Golf Club for some years. He was a keen cricketer and played for the Gentlemen of Shropshire and also played rugby for *Moseley Rugby Club*. On the Moseley memorial it lists his name as C.R. Venables and so the third name is also speculation! There are three Venables on the Hall of Memory site but none are possible. There is only one C. Venables listed on the Commonwealth war graves site and he is a Corporal from Shropshire.

To add to further confusion the Commonwealth War Graves Commission has him listed as being a member of the 3rd Battalion. As this was a Reserve Battalion kept in Britain for the duration of the War is doesn't fit with what happened to Gilbert. The possibility is that he started off in the 3rd Battalion and then was transferred to the 2nd Battalion, indeed he is listed as such at the Oswestry Golf Club. The 2nd Battalion was a Regular battalion, serving in India from 1903-14. It soon mobilised for war and joined 80th Brigade, 27th Division. It went to France, on 21st December 1914 and then went to the Ypres Salient which was in constant attack from the German forces which surrounded the Salient. Whilst serving in the trenches Gilbert was shot through the heart by a sniper. He died aged 34 on *7th March 1915* and is buried in the Voormezeele Enclosure grave number 3 1. A. 2.

4. Lieutenant Frederick Bonham Burr – 3rd Battalion Worcestershire Regiment. He was born on 2nd August 1887 in Blacklands, Hastings, Sussex, the son of Rev. G.F. and Caroline Burr of Highfields Park, Halesowen. He was educated at Sandroyd, Cobham, at Denstone College and at Keble College, Oxford. He played a single first-class game, for Worcestershire against Oxford University in 1911 and made 39 and 7 not out, and caught Ronald Lagden in the first innings. He  played cricket for *Ashfield Cricket Club*. He wrote a collection of poems called 'The Strummings of a Lyre' in 1912 and was preparing for Holy Orders when war was declared. He was in the Territorial Force being a member of the 6th Battalion Worcestershire Regiment but went out as an officer in the 3rd Battalion.

The Battle of Neuve Chapelle began on 10th March 1915 and lasted until 13th March. On 12th March 1915 the 3rd Battalion Worcestershire Regiment marched from Loire and occupied assembly trenches in preparation for an attack on the German position at the Spanbroek Mill, Lindenhoek, Belgium. There were 2 companies of Worcestershire Regiment on the right and 2 companies of Wiltshire Regiment on the left. The assault was to begin at 8.40am but was postponed due to fog and so the troops stood in wet trenches all morning until the fog cleared sufficiently and then the artillery bombardment commenced at 2.30pm with the assault being ordered for 4.10pm.

When the attack began they came under heavy rifle and machine gun fire, the latter principally from the front and the right front causing heavy casualties. Despite this a party of about 40 were able to occupy a portion of the front German trench. Another group sheltered in some ruined buildings and were just about to make a dash for the German trench to support the gains when our own artillery unfortunately dropped a high explosive shell in these buildings killing and wounding a number and scattering the remainder. The party holding the trench managed to hold on for 3 hours until they were ordered to withdraw under cover of darkness. They succeeded in bringing away all the wounded from the German trench. Under cover of darkness the Battalion was withdrawn and returned to Locre. 1 captain, 1 Lieutenant and 7 2nd Lieutenants were killed, which were all the officers of A company, and 38 other ranks. 32 were missing believed killed and 99 were wounded. He died on the *12th March 1915* aged 28 and is buried in the Kemmel Chateau Military Cemetery.

5. Captain John Francis – "D" Company 1st /5th Battalion Royal Warwickshire. He was the son of John and Ethel Francis, of 7, Westbourne Road, Birmingham. He was educated at Uppingham School and Gottingen, Germany. He played rugby at Uppingham and joined *Moseley Rugby Club* where he was described as '... of fine physique and stood close on six feet, was a sturdy forward. Of a genial and bright disposition he was a general favourite.' He was also a member of the Edgbaston Golf Club. He was a Director and Secretary of Deakin & Francis, Manufacturing jewellers. He joined the 5th Territorial Battalion of the Warwickshire Regiment as soon as it was inaugurated in April 1908 and was promoted to 2nd Lieutenant and then Lieutenant in the same Regiment in October 1909. When war began he was promoted to Captain and was given command of D Company. The Battalion was mobilised for war on the 22nd March 1915 and landed at Havre where they became the 143rd Brigade of the 48th Division. They were involved in the 2nd Battle of Ypres from 21st April to

23rd May during which the Germans used gas on a large scale for the first time. They remained in the Ypres Salient. Whilst on duty in the trenches on the Ales-sines Road near Ploegrsteert he was shot by a sniper and killed. He died on *2nd June 1915* aged 27 and is buried in the Berks Cemetery Extension.

The Colonel of the Battalion wrote: 'It was the officers of the type of Johnny Francis, as he was known in the mess, that made the regiment what it was. Francis loved the regiment, loved his company, and his men were devoted to him. Amidst 30 or 40 officers there are bound to be degrees of character, force and capacity, but in Francis I had the perfect soldier. As to character, he was the soul of honour, a disciplined officer, a true friend. He had a keen sense of justice and a rough sort of loving kindness to his men which made them value him. As to force, he was a born commander, a leader of men. As to capabilities, he was clever, knew his job thoroughly and had a way of imparting knowledge to his men, and he was hard-working; he was never idle. As to courage, there never was a braver man. He was not merely a brave fool who saw no danger. I think he was the kind of man who enjoyed danger. He would take a fearful punishment on the football field or in a boxing match with the utmost good temper. There was about him a joyous courage. I doubted some men's courage, I doubted my own, but I never doubted his.'

6. Captain Norman Kingsley Street – 9th Battalion Worcestershire Regiment. He was born in Edgbaston in 1881 and was the only son of T.R. Street of Lea Croft, Kidderminster and formerly of Edgbaston Birmingham. He attended Bromsgrove School 1896-1900. He was a School Monitor and a member of both the rugby XV and was captain of the cricket team. He was described as a 'sterling forward' and a 'hard-hitter' with the bat. He was a right-handed batsman and played 5 first class  matches for Warwickshire in the 1908 season. He was an opening bat and in his 9 innings he scored 43 runs. At some point he played rugby for *Moseley Rugby Club*. After school he went to Sandhurst and became a 2nd Lieutenant in the 4th Battalion Worcestershire Regiment. In 1910 he was attached to the West African Frontier Force.

With stalemate on the Western Front, as the troops became bogged down in trench warfare, alternative theatres of war were considered. In 1915 a plan was devised to knock Turkey out of the War by attacking through the Gallipoli Peninsular. The initial attacks in April 1915 had been a total failure and a further attack further up the peninsular was planned for August 1915. The 9th Battalion Worcestershire Regiment left Blackdown on Salisbury Plain on Sunday 20th June 1915 and moved by train to Avonmouth. There, on the same evening, the transport ship, Cawdor Castle, received the Battalion, 28 officers and 970 other ranks. They were part of the 13th Division and in the 39th

Brigade. Street was the Staff Captain for the Brigade. After a long journey they reached the Gallipoli peninsular on 13th July. Here they found the same deadlock as on the Western Front. The new plan of attack was to strike the Turks at Suvla Bay. The 13th Division has been purposely landed at Helles in the south to mislead the Turks into thinking that the attack would come from there. The 9th battalion remained in the trenches at Helles until the end of July and suffered their first casualties. On 29th July the 13th Division was withdrawn to Lemnos in order to take part in the decisive attack of the forthcoming offensive. The 13th Division, including the 9th Worcestershire were selected for the decisive attack at Sari Bair, whilst a subsidiary attack of the 29th Division at Krithia was to involve the 4th Worcestershire. The Allied landings began on 6th August 1915 but immediately ran into trouble with the troops been landed at the wrong places, unnecessary delays allowing the Turks to strengthen their positions and hostile terrain which favoured the defenders. The attacks foundered in the gullies and ravines. The local Turkish commander, Mustafa Kemal, poured in reinforcements, with the result that two heavy counter-attacks were launched on the 10th August from the commanding height of Chunuk Bair. Street and his men took the brunt of one of these attacks. A 'position had been lost and a crowd of men had stuck halfway in an effort to re-take it. And a critical situation had arisen. He volunteered to go to get them in and had succeeded in bringing them right up to the position before he fell.' He died aged 34 on *10th August 1915* and is remembered on the Helles Memorial.

7. Lance Corporal Edward Thomas Blackham (there are no F B on the Commonwealth War Graves Commission site and the only F is Canadian) 2192 Queen's Own Worcestershire Hussars (Worcester Yeomanry). He was the son of Alderman Arthur and Rosa Blackham, of 173, Woodlands Road, Sparkhill, Birmingham. He was educated at King Edward's, Camp Hill. He was a keen cricketer and was a prominent member of the Camp Hill Old Boys' Club and also played for *Ashfield Cricket Club* and *Moor Green Football Club*. He was a partner in the firm of Messrs. Blackham and Powell, Paper Box Manufacturers. (There is another possibility later in the book).

Before the war he had been associated with the Worcestershire Yeomanry for some time before the war broke out. His Battalion was sent to the Gallipoli Peninsula after being stationed at Alexandria for some months. He was killed aged 25 on *28th August 1915* when he was hit by a shrapnel bullet. He is buried in Green Hill Cemetery.

8. 2nd Lieutenant George Walter Field – 10th Battalion Gloucestershire Regiment. He was the son of Arthur and Florence Field, of Fairfield, Yardley Wood Road, Moseley, Birmingham. He was educated at King Edward's, Camp Hill. He played football for *Moor Green Football Club*. After leaving school he was a pupil to Mr W. Bowater, dentist, Broad Street, Birmingham.

When war began he enlisted in 14th Battalion (1st Battalion Birmingham Pals) Royal Warwickshire Regiment but was commissioned in the Gloucester Regiment. He went to France with his battalion in August 1915 and was involved in the Battle of Loos (25th September to 16th October 1915). This was the first genuinely large scale British offensive action in support of a larger French attack in the Third Battle of Artois. Before the attack began the British commanders had complained that the ground over which they were being called upon to advance was wholly unsuitable with coal mines and slag heaps. This was the first use of gas by the British but unfortunately its effect was somewhat negated as the wind blew it back to their own lines. Despite heavy casualties, there was considerable success on the first day in breaking into the deep enemy positions near Loos and Hulluch. Unfortunately Field was one of those killed. He died on *25th September 1915* aged 19 and is buried in the St. Mary's A.D.S. Cemetery, Haisnes.

9. Lance Corporal Charles Leonard Ovens 11421 'A' Company 2nd Battalion Oxford and Bucks Light Infantry (52nd Foot). He was the only son of Charles Leonard and Elizabeth Ann Ovens, of 18, Ophir Terrace, Ann's Hill Road, Brockhurst, Gosport, Hampshire and was born on 18th June 1890 in Peckham, London. He was educated at the Royal Marines Light Infantry School in Gosport and then at the Leesland School where he was a pupil teacher for

two years. He then went to the Burough Road College, Isleworth. He became a teacher at the City Elementary School in Birmingham. He was a first class athlete and was associated with both the Birmingham and *Moseley Rugby Club*.

He enlisted on the 2nd September 1914 and after nine weeks training he went to France where he took part in the fighting at Ypres, Richebourg and

Festubert. His Battalion was also involved in the first day of the attack at the Battle of Loos and suffered heavy casualties. He was offered a commission but declined preferring to remain in the ranks. He was killed at Givenchy aged 25 on *25th September 1915*. His Captain wrote: 'I was very sorry that your son was killed in the fight on 25th September. He was a most awfully good fellow in every way, and I know that he will be missed by all of us who knew him out there.' Company Quartermaster Sergeant A. Beare wrote: 'He was always the same, so cheery under any circumstances and absolutely fearless. You may know the details of how he got killed; be consoled that he knew no pain. He went into the charge on the German trench, and got right to the parapet when he received a bullet in the left side and he lived about two minutes. He died a glorious death for his country.' He is remembered on the Loos Memorial. He doesn't appear on the *Moseley Rugby Club* Memorial.

10. 2nd Lieutenant Douglas Howard Wilson Greenway – 13th Battalion Worcestershire Regiment, attached to the 4th Battalion. He was the second son of Herbert and Emily Greenway, of 64, Greenhill Road, Moseley, Birmingham. His father was a pewter and brass founder. He was educated at Oundle School, Northamptonshire. After leaving school Douglas joined his father's business as a clerk and then worked as secretary at Messrs Gaskell and Chambers Limited, Dale End, Birmingham. In his leisure time he played golf and was a member of *Moseley Golf Club*. He was a skilful golfer and well-known in Midland and Welsh golf circles.

When war began he enlisted in 14th Battalion (1st Battalion Birmingham Pals) Royal Warwickshire Regiment. He was commissioned in the Worcestershire Regiment on 19th February 1915 and went to Gallipoli with his Battalion. Following the Suvla Bay landings the fighting became the

familiar struggle of attack and counter attack with few gains made. Greenway died a hero's death. On the night of 17th October 1915 the Battalion was in the front line and were tasked with repairing damage to their trenches and protective barbed wire. As a precaution a small covering party had been sent forward to ensure the safety of workers but it was they who came under fire and three men were wounded. Greenway volunteered to bring back the wounded men. He crawled out under three belts of barbed wire with enemy fire over his head. He dragged two of the men back to safety but was himself killed as he attempted to bring back the third. He died aged 24 on *17th October 1915* and is buried in the Azmak Cemetery, Suvla. In 1923 his father presented the Greenway Bowl to Moseley Golf Club in memory of his son.

Chapter 4

1916

1916 began with plans for a big and hopefully decisive joint action between the British and the French. Unfortunately the Germans had their own plans hoping to 'bleed the French white' at Verdun. This meant that the British had to take on a far larger portion of the offensive.

11. Staff Quartermaster Sergeant Maurice William Hobson – 325015 Queen's Own Worcestershire Hussars (Worcester Yeomanry). He was the youngest son of Mr George Hobson, Grove Avenue, Moseley. His father was a manager for Norwich Union. Maurice was educated at King Edward's School, New Street, Birmingham. Whilst at school he played for the 2 XV for rugby but doesn't appear to have played cricket. He remedied this by becoming a key member of the *Ashfield Cricket Club* and  he also played for *Moor Green Football Club*. On leaving school he was employed as a commercial traveller for a brass founders and then worked as an engineer.

He had been in the Worcestershire Yeomanry for about 9 years before the War and was immediately mobilized when war was declared in August 1914 and enlisted as a sergeant in the Worcester Yeomanry. They were in the Kings Lynn area in January 1915. On the 19th January 1915 the Germans launched their first air raid on Britain when they attacked Kings Lynn and Great Yarmouth causing deaths. The Earl of Dudley, the Colonel of the Regiment, presented Maurice with a riding whip following the air raid and the Countess presented him with a Pear Blossom Badge and so one can only assume that he had done some act of bravery. He was promoted to Quartermaster Sergeant. The Regiment was sent to Egypt in April 1915 and then in August took part in the Suvla Bay landings. Casualties due to fighting and sickness led to them being temporarily merged with 1/1st Gloucestershire and 1/1st Warwickshire Yeomanry to form the 1st South Midlands Regiment, 1st Composite Mounted Brigade. At the end of December 1915 they were evacuated to Mudros and then were sent back to Egypt. They went to Mena Camp close to the Pyramids. In February, after trekking 20 miles over sand they arrived at Kantara. Here the countryside was nothing but desert, covered with fine, deep sand, formidable for horses and infantry alike. They spent their time patrolling the other side of the Suez Canal. They spent three weeks there without seeing the Turks. In early April, whilst out on reconnaissance, they were attacked by a combined Turk and Bedouin force. They managed to stem the attack and both sides retreated. After this the Brigade was sent to Katia 25 miles east of the Suez Canal to guard a newly constructed railway.

On 21st April a party of 50 sappers were sent to sink wells as Oghratina, some five miles north east in the Sinai Desert where a grove of palm trees lay at the foot of a steep, horseshoe shaped hill. This was a very isolated position and a detachment of Worcester Yeomanry, about 180 strong, were sent to protect them. The early morning of 23rd April 1916, which was Easter Sunday, opened with fog and with visibility not more than 20 yards. At 4.15am camels were heard moving and all ranks moved to their posts. When they could make out figures rifle fire was directed towards them. Unfortunately they had alerted a passing group of about 2 to 3,000 Turkish infantry who immediately began to attack the position. The first attack was repulsed but a second attack was made from the south-east and the Yeomanry were thinned out and they were pushed back by the weight of the onslaught so that the survivors were left defending the crest of the hill until they were forced to surrender. Only four officers and forty-two other ranks survived. Maurice was not among them. He died aged 27 on *23rd April 1916* and is remembered on the Jerusalem Memorial.

12. 2nd Lieutenant Philip Leslie Patterson 1st Battalion North Staffordshire Regiment was born in Acocks Green in 1894, the youngest son and eighth of the nine children of parents William Ernest Patterson, a manufacturing jeweller, and his wife, Annie, who lived at the Ards, Knowle. He was educated at St Chad's, Prestatyn, North Wales and then at Warwick School. He played rugby for *Moseley Rugby Club* and cricket for Knowle & Dorridge Cricket Club.

He joined the 6th Battalion, Royal Warwickshire Regiment in September 1914, and went to France in March 1915. He was commissioned in August 1915, and was posted to the 1st Battalion North Staffordshire Regiment. He was killed in action near Wulverghem, Belgium, aged 21, on *4th June 1916*.

13. 2nd Lieutenant John Balkwill – 6th Battalion Royal Warwickshire Regiment. He was the son of Francis and Mary Vince Balkwill, of Forest Hill, London. He was born in 1883, the 4th of five children. He was educated at St Dunstan's College, Catford, London from 1893-1899. At St. Dunstan's he was Captain of Athletics, and played in the Rugby 1st XV, Lacrosse 1st XII, and Cricket 1st XI. On leaving school in 1899 he was employed as an insurance clerk at the  London office of the Northern Assurance Company. In July 1908, the company transferred him to their Birmingham office as a surveyor, and he took up residence in Moseley before moving to Dorridge where he was a keen and enthusiastic member of Knowle Cricket Club. He was also a member of *Ashfield Cricket Club* and may also have played for *Moor Green Football Club*.

On the outbreak of war, John enlisted in the 6th Battalion Royal Warwickshire Regiment as a Private. He went to France on 22nd March 1915 and was promoted to corporal and then was commissioned in the same Battalion as a Second Lieutenant on 19th September 1915. He was killed on the first day of the Battle of the Somme, 1st July 1916. The 6th Battalion were in the second wave of the attack, going over the top 10 minutes after the first and no doubt climbing over many dead bodies. The 6th Battalion soon found itself in difficulties, as the German counter bombardment was by now ploughing up no-man's land and they were met with a hail of machine gun and rifle fire. Those units that had managed to advance into the German trenches, now found that they were not only cut off from reinforcements to help push forwards but also hindered from going back. The 6th Battalion suffered horrendous casualties with 10 officers killed as well as many other ranks. John was among the dead. He died aged 33 on *1st July 1916* and is buried in Pargny British Cemetery.

14. 2nd Lieutenant Frank Aldridge Fawcett – 1st/5th Battalion South Staffordshire Regiment. He was the only child of Frederick and Eva Fawcett. He was born in 1896. In 1911 the family were living in 32 Springfield Road,

Kings Heath, Birmingham. He was an ex-pupil of King Edward's School. He played cricket for *Ashfield Cricket Club*.

When the War began he joined the 14th Battalion Royal Warwickshire Regiment (1st Birmingham Pals) as Private 14/236 before being promoted to Sergeant and then to 2nd Lieutenant in September 1915. He joined the 1st/5th South Staffordshire Regiment. After a short spell in Egypt he went to France with his unit where he worked as a battalion bombing officer. On the first day of the Battle of the Somme the Battalion were ordered to attack the north side of the Gommecourt Salient. This was intended as a diversionary attack for the main attack a few miles south. The attack was a disaster as the British guns had made little impression on the barbed wire and also on the deeply dug German positions. The result was that the Battalion was cut to pieces by a mixture of rifle and machine gun fire and shrapnel shells. The 46th Division suffered with 50 officers killed and 71 wounded, 803 other ranks killed and 1340 wounded. They were categorised unfairly as '... showing lack of offensive spirit'! Frank was recorded as missing during an attack. He died aged 19 on *1st July 1916* and is remembered on the Thiepval Memorial.

15. Lieutenant Harold Egbert Foizey – 18th Battalion West Yorkshire Regiment (Prince of Wales's Own). He was born in 1885 and was the son of Benjamin and Alice Foizey, of Tipton, Staffs, and an ex-pupil of King Edward's School, New Street, Birmingham. He played cricket for *Ashfield Cricket Club*. He was working for Messrs. Stewarts & Lloyds (Ltd), Iron and Steel Manufacturers of Neville Street, Leeds when the war started.

He joined the 15th Battalion (1st Leeds Pals), The Prince of Wales's Own (West Yorkshire Regiment), Private [15/343], on the outbreak of war. He then became a Lance Corporal and in May 1915 was commissioned in the 18th Battalion (2nd Bradford Pals) West Yorkshire Regiment (Prince of Wales's Own). In December 1915 they went to Alexandria to defend the Suez Canal and then in March 1916 they left Port Said for France. Their first taste of action was at Serre on the first day of the Battle of the Somme, 1st July 1916. At half-past seven in the morning the Bradford Pals emerged from the trenches to find barbed wire not cut, and German machine guns not silenced. The machine guns cut them down in waves. The soldiers stumbled forward over their dead colleagues only to be cut down themselves. By the end of the day 1,770 were dead. An account published in the *Yorkshire Evening Post*, of 10th July 1916, quotes a letter written to Foizey's sister by a fellow officer it reads: 'I saw Lieutenant Foizey tumble over the back of a trench, wounded in the thigh, I made him comfortable, and had his wounds dressed, and placed him in a traverse at the back of the trench, soon afterwards a terrible explosion took place, throwing up all the sandbags and earthwork, in the immediate neighbourhood, and burying several men, together with Lieutenant Foizey, underneath.' Later, when trench repairs were taking place, his body was recovered and he was given a burial. He died on *1st July 1916* aged 31 and is buried in Euston Road Cemetery, Colincamps.

16. 2nd Lieutenant William Henry Furse – 21st (Tyneside Scottish) Battalion Northumberland Fusiliers. He was the eldest son of Henry and Florence Mundy Furse, of Cragside, School Road, Moseley and later of 36, Salisbury Road, Moseley, Birmingham. The family came from London before settling in Moseley where the maternal grandmother lived. Both William and his brother Alan went to Solihull School and both played cricket for *Ashfield Cricket Club*. William also played for *Moor Green Football Club*. He was a clerk in Lloyds Bank, Stirchley. He married Miss Beatrice Law of Cambridge Road, Kings Heath in October 1915.

When war was declared he joined the 14th Battalion Royal Warwickshire Regiment (1st Birmingham Pals), Private 14/399, rising to the rank of sergeant in April 1915. He was then commissioned in the 21st Battalion (2nd Tyneside Scottish) Northumberland Fusiliers in September 1915. They landed in France in January 1916 and were involved in the Battle of the Somme. On 1st July 1916 they were in the front line in Sausage Valley. Their task on the day was to capture the German front line and then other Battalions would move through them. After the massive bombardment a huge mine was detonated at Lochnagar at 0728 hours. Two minutes later the whistles were blown and the British troops emerged from the trenches. William was in charge of a trench mortar battery. The opposing trenches were close together with No Man's Land pitted with shell holes. At 6 feet and 5½ inches he was said to be the tallest man in the British Army and therefore an easy target.

The German machine guns tore into the British forces. Apparently William stopped to light his pipe, and was then hit by a bullet and was mortally wounded. He was taken back to the British lines but died soon afterwards. He died aged 25 on *1st July 1916* and is buried in Bapaume Post Military Cemetery, Albert.

17. 2nd Lieutenant William Worthington Sanby – 20th (Tyneside Scottish) Battalion Northumberland Fusiliers. He was the son of Arthur Hill Sanby and Ellen Sanby. He was born on 9th August 1895, and was admitted to King Edward's School, New Street in January 1909, having transferred from Woodroughs School in Moseley. He was the youngest of nine children. His father, Arthur, was a commercial traveller for a sewing cotton manufacturer. The family had a number of addresses including 'Ivanhoe', St. Agnes Road, Moseley; The Gables, Stratford-on-Avon; Nellfield, Hartopp Road, Four Oaks and Hazelwell Hall, Kings Heath. He played football for *Moor Green Football Club.*

He joined the 14th Battalion (1st Birmingham Pals) Royal Warwickshire Regiment at the start of the war and was Lance Corporal 764. On 16th April 1915 he was commissioned in the Northumberland Fusiliers. He went to France in January 1916 with his path being the same as William Furse's Battalion. On 1st July 1916 they attacked at La Boisselle over the 800 yards of No Man's Land in Mash Valley. William and the majority of his battalion were cut down by machine gun fire and although a few isolated parties made the front line they were ultimately all killed. William's body was never recovered, but he is commemorated on the Thiepval Memorial. He died aged 21 on *1st July 1916* and is remembered on the Thiepval Memorial.

18. ? On the Ashfield Memorial he is just referred to as **G. Davis**. There are ten possibilities with Birmingham connections and so this is just a guess. *Private George Albert Davis* 2nd Battalion (Duke of Edinburgh's) Wiltshire Regiment. William and Ada Davis, of 2, Bishopsgate Terrace, Bishopsgate Street, Birmingham and husband of Florence Davis, of 10/141, Cooksey Road, Small Heath, Birmingham. He played for *Moor Green Football Club.*

Prior to joining the Wiltshire Regiment he was 1067 Royal Warwickshire Regiment. This would imply that he was previously wounded and then drafted into the Wiltshire Regiment who had taken horrendous casualties at Neuve Chappelle in March 1915. The 2nd Battalion started 1916 in the area of Amiens. They remained in this general area relieving units in trenches and training for an offensive that was going to take place in July. On the 1st July they were in support in the area of Montauban, followed by two days of attacks. They remained in this area for most of July. On the 8th July they played a leading part in the attack on Trones Wood and at one point bayoneted their way through what remained of the German defenders in the wood. They suffered 240 casualties in this action but were awarded plus 23 decorations for gallantry. He died of wounds on *8th July 1916*.

19. Captain George Pendrell Blake – 10th Battalion Royal Welsh Fusiliers. He was born on 23rd January 1879 and was the son of Dr George Farncombe and Mary Elizabeth Blake, of Bishopstone, 2 Cambridge Road, Kings Heath, Birmingham. He went to Malvern College where he was captain of cricket and a keen member of the Officer Training Corps. He went to Trinity College, Cambridge and left in 1901. He became Assistant Master at Merchiston Castle School, Edinburgh 1903-5 and then at Bradfield College, Berkshire. He was a member of *Moseley Golf Club*.

When the war began he volunteered to fight and was offered a commission in the 10th Battalion (Service) the Royal Welsh Fusiliers as a temporary Captain. They went to France on 27th September 1915 and were part of the 76th Brigade, 3rd Division. They were concentrated in the Ypres sector. On the 18th February 1916 George was injured by shrapnel and was taken to the Red Cross Hospital at Le Touquet and then sent home for treatment eventually reaching the 1st Southern General Hospital at Birmingham University on 30th March 1916 and then was passed fit. He arrived back in France on 31st May. The Battalion was sent to the Somme Sector but did not take part in the Battle until 14th July at Bazentine Ridge. On 19th July 1916 they were in the attack at Delville Wood. At midnight on the 20th July, the 10th Battalion were ordered to take positions in Delville Wood with the aim being to clear the Germans from this stronghold. There had been no previous reconnaissance and the 10th Battalion were instructed to make their way by compass bearing. They were to meet a guide to their position and no shots were to be fired because there were South African troops in the area. Unfortunately shots were fired and the Germans sent up Very Lights followed by machine gun and rifle fire. The battalion dug in and then were ordered to attack at 3.45 but were repulsed and found themselves under attack. They held on and were relieved almost a day after the attack began at 3.26am. 119 were wounded and 50 unaccounted for including George who was killed along with 3 other officers and 35 other ranks. He died aged 37 on *20th July 1916* and is buried in the A.I.F. Burial Ground, Flers.

20. Corporal Ernest Clifford Hill – 371 14th Battalion Royal Warwickshire Regiment. He was the second son of Walter Benjamin and Ann Elizabeth Hill, of 18, Cambridge Road, Kings Heath, Birmingham. He went to King Edward's, Camp Hill where he played both rugby and cricket. He was a prominent member with his brother, Howard, of *Ashfield Cricket Club*. They also joined *Moseley Rugby Club* where they were key members of the pre-war team. Ernest and Howard, along with their friend Austin Woodward, also played for the Midland Counties team. He worked as a printer's assistant.

At the outbreak of war he joined the 14th Battalion (1st Birmingham Pals) Royal Warwickshire Regiment which was formed by the Lord Mayor in September 1914. There followed training, first at Sutton Park, then in Wensley Dale and finally on Salisbury Plain. On 21st November they were mobilised for war and landed at Boulogne. They became involved in the Battle of the Somme in July. They were part of the attack on High Wood on the night of 22nd/23rd July. The Germans had regained most of the wood after twice almost being in the hands of the British and held the Pommiers Redoubt. The 14th Battalion along with 1st Royal West Kents attacked the south-eastern part of the wood and Wood Lane whilst the 4th Gordon Highlanders attacked the eastern corner

of the wood. There was a preliminary bombardment but this wasn't sufficient to cause sufficient casualties amongst the Germans who caused awful casualties amongst the attacking forces. No sufficient gains were made and the attack was called off. The Royal West Kents suffered 420 casualties. The 14th Warwickshires were also decimated with 194 casualties. Edward was amongst those killed. He died aged 23 on *23rd July 1916* and is remembered on the Thiepval Memorial.

21. Private William Ernest Stubbs – 996 14th Battalion Royal Warwickshire Regiment. He was the son of William Henry and Ida Alice Stubbs, of 121, Poplar Avenue, Edgbaston, Birmingham. His father was a solicitor. He was born on 24th October 1895, was admitted to King Edward's School on 21st September 1909, having previously attended Cambridge House School, Lyttleton Road, Edgbaston. His school record does not show him in the rugby or cricket teams and so I suspect that his appearance on the Ashfield Memorial probably means that he played for *Moor Green Football Club*. After leaving school in 1911, he became a bank clerk at the Acocks Green branch of Lloyds Bank.

In 1914, William enlisted in the 14th Battalion (1st Birmingham Pals) Royal Warwickshire Regiment. The Battalion landed at Boulogne on 21st November 1915 and William spent his entire military career in France. His military career would be the same as Ernest Hill and so, unfortunately, his death. He was reported missing on *23rd July 1916*, later presumed killed, aged 20. As his body was never recovered, William is commemorated on the Thiepval Memorial.

22. Private John Edward Chilton Price 14/295 "B" Company 14th Battalion Royal Warwickshire Regiment. Eldest son of Charles E. and Louisa Price, 86 Balsall Heath Road, Edgbaston, Birmingham. In 1911 he was an insurance clerk. I suspect that he played football for *Moor Green Football Club* but also cricket for *Ashfield Cricket Club*.

He died aged 24 on 23rd July 1916, Longueval. He joined up at the start of the war and his military career would have followed that of Ernest and William as did his death on *23rd July 1916*, aged 24. He is buried in Caterpillar Valley Cemetery.

23. Private George Joseph Griffiths – 15/1528 15th Battalion Royal Warwickshire Regiment. He was the son of Mr. and Mrs. Henry Griffiths of 8, Princess Road, Edgbaston, Birmingham. He played for *Ashfield Cricket Club* and *Moor Green Football Club*.

15th (2nd Birmingham Pals) Battalion, The Royal Warwickshire Regiment was raised in Birmingham in September 1914. They moved south in July to reinforce the British forces on the Somme. They were involved in the attack on High Wood on the night of 22nd/23rd July. They moved to their trenches at 9pm. These were shallow old German trenches which ran along the Longueval-Bazentin Le Grand Road. As they waited they could see their barrage pulverising the German lines. On their left they could see Delville Wood on fire. They attacked after the West Kents and the 14th Battalion had begun their attack. They went forward across the chaos of the battlefield over rising ground and in the dark. The Germans opened fire with rifle and machine gun fire scything through the advancing forces. Men took cover where best they could as the attack was halted and eventually retired. The 15th Battalion suffered 141 casualties with 34 killed including Percy Jeeves, the Warwickshire County Cricket Club player, whose name was used by P.G. Wodehouse in his stories. George was also amongst those who died. He died aged 22 on *23rd July 1916* and is remembered on the Thiepval Memorial.

24. 2nd Lieutenant Rowland Evan Basil Rowlands – 16th Battalion (3rd Birmingham Pals) Royal Warwickshire Regiment. He was the son of Basil and Linda Rowland. In 1911 he was single and working as an Assistant Master at Greenhill School, Moseley. He was born in Sutton Coldfield. His mother moved to Yorkshire after the war, living at 25 St. Paul's Square, York. He played for *Moor Green Football Club*.

He enlisted in September 1914 joining the last of the three Birmingham Pals Battalions, the 16th Battalion, and was given the rank of sergeant and then promoted to 2nd Lieutenant. They proceeded to France on 21st November 1915. They were transferred to the 15th Brigade 5th Division. In March 1916 the 5th Division took over a section of the front line between St. Laurent Blangy and the southern edge of Vimy Ridge, near Arras. On the 13th July they moved south to reinforce the attack in the Battle of the Somme. They marched along hot and dusty roads in a series of night marches reaching their destination on 16th July. They were deployed Lahoussoye-Bresle-Ribemont-Heilly, a few miles south of Albert. On the 18th July the 5th Division came under orders of the XV Corps of the British Fourth Army. In the planned attack the 5th Division's objective was to take the high ground between High Wood and Delville Wood. The 16th were concentrated on the Mametz-Montauban road. On the 23rd July the 16th were placed in reserve and took over positions along the slopes around the quarry along the eastern end of Caterpillar Valley.

On the 27th July, at 7.10am, the British Fourth Army resumed their offensive upon Longueval and Delville Wood. The guns opened up from both sides with hot metal filling the air and the ground peppered with blasts. The 16th Battalion attacked with a creeping barrage for the first time against an enemy well dug in and making use of the numerous fortified cellars in Longueval. Bitter fighting followed as both sides fought from fortified point to fortified point. The Battalion lost 267 soldiers, with 57 killed and 45 never recovered. Captain James Holmes recorded that he met Rowland at the edge of the wood. He told him that he was quite certain that he was going to be killed. Holmes tried to cheer him up. Holmes moved away and when he came back to where Rowland was with his men there was a big shell hole and no sign of Rowland. He died aged 26 on *27th July 1916* and is remembered on the Thiepval Memorial.

25. Captain William Herbert Hedges MC – 1st (North Midland) Field Company, Royal Engineers. He was born in 1893 and was the son of William and Emily Hedges of 117, Anderton Park Road, Moseley, Birmingham. He attended Wintersloe School in Moseley from 1905 to 1907 and then went to Malvern College. Afterwards he entered the firm of Hedges Limited (Chemists), Dale End, Birmingham, becoming a director just before the war started. He was well-known and popular in athletic circles being prominently identified with Moseley Cricket Club and Birmingham Athletic Club as well as playing rugby for *Moseley Rugby Club* and golf at *Moseley Golf Club*. He also excelled at boxing and won both the middle-weight and heavy-weight championships of the West Midlands. In 1914 he had played for Moseley Cricket Club against Warwickshire County Cricket Club at the County Ground at Edgbaston. On the opposing side was Percy Jeeves.

When war broke out he was commissioned as 2nd Lieutenant in the 1st (North Midland) Field Company, North Midland Divisional Engineers Royal Engineers. They went to France on 23rd February 1915. He was wounded in April 1915 and was sent back for treatment in England. On returning to active service in October 1915, he was promoted to acting Captain. In December 1915 his Division was sent to Egypt but was there for just a few days when their orders were changed and they went back to France. In June 1916 he received the news that he had been awarded the Military Cross for rescuing two injured men in 1915. On 1st July 1916 his Company was involved in the first day of the Battle of the Somme. William survived that first day but was severely wounded later in the Battle on 18th August 1916. He died from his injuries three days later on *22nd August 1916*. He was 23 years old. He is buried in Warlincourt Halte British Cemetery, Saulty, France.

26. Private Phillip Reeves Vaughton – 6544 1st/14th Battalion London Scottish Regiment. He was born in Edgbaston in 1893 and attended Bromsgrove School from 1907 to 1910. He played rugby for *Moseley Rugby Club*. He was in business in South Africa before the war.

He joined the London Scottish on his return to England and went to France in 1916. The 14th Battalion were a territorial unit and had been in action since October 1914. The original members of the Battalion would have been severely depleted by the time that Phillip joined them. Their first action of 1916 was the first day of the Somme, 1st July. They were involved in the diversionary attack on Gommecourt. At 7.30am, on 1 July, the attack on Gommecourt began and the 56th (1st London) Division to the south, overran the first two German trenches. Troops also reached the third trench but a strongpoint at Nameless Farm held out despite several attacks. The German artillery fired a standing barrage along no man's land and trapped the British on the far side all day as German infantry gradually recaptured the lost trenches, all attempts to send reinforcements from the British lines being costly failures. The parties who got across no man's land were surrounded and destroyed, a few men being taken prisoner. One of those taken prisoner was Phillip who was severely wounded. He was taken to a German hospital and died on *2nd September 1916*. He is buried in the Niederzwehren Prisoner of War Cemetery.

27. Lance Corporal Charles Chester Illingworth – 74 15th Battalion (2nd Birmingham Pals) Royal Warwickshire Regiment. He was born in Yorkshire on 15th October 1896 to Charles and Martha Illingworth. The family moved to 71 Cartland Road, Stirchley, Birmingham where Charles attended Kings Norton Boys School. His father was captain of Kings Heath Cricket Club and so we can assume that he played cricket for them as he is remembered on their  roll of honour. Whether his loyalty to his father meant that he didn't play cricket for Ashfield is possible and so it is likely that he played football for *Moor Green Football Club*. On leaving school he began work at the Bristol Street, Birmingham branch of Lloyds Bank.

When the War started he joined the 15th Battalion as many of his friends would do. Once in France the Battalion was pitched into the Battle of the Somme fighting almost continuously from the 17th July 1916 and then through the rest of July and August. On 3rd September his Division, the 5th, was involved in the Battle of Guillemont (3rd-6th September 1916). Guillemont was on the right flank of the British line since the middle of July and had been continuously attacked without success during August. This Battle was intended to finally capture it. It was essential to capture it if the French and British were to cooperate properly north of the Somme which would then lead to attacks on Flers and Courcelette. The 5th Division were on the right of this attack with their target being Leuze Wood, 1,500 yards beyond the village, on a ridge overlooking the village of Combles. There were heavy casualties as the troops advanced through murderous rifle and machine gun fire. Despite this the 5th Division captured its first three objectives, and reached a line east of Guillemont. He died aged 20 on *3rd September 1916* and is remembered on the Thiepval Memorial.

28. Private William Anthony Machin – PS/2035 16th Battalion Middlesex Regiment. He was the son of Frank T. and R.E. Machin, of 59, Salisbury Road, Moseley, Birmingham. He attended Solihull School. On leaving school he became a commercial traveller for a paper manufacturer. He played football for *Moor Green Football Club*.

The 16th (Public Schools) Battalion, Middlesex Regiment (Duke of Cambridge's Own) was raised in London on the 1st of September 1914 by Lt-Col. J.J. Mackay. Amongst the recruits were enough former international players for the Battalion to field two rugby union teams and one football team. They joined 100th Brigade, 33rd Division at Clipstone Camp in July and moved to Perham Down for final training in August 1915. They proceeded to France on the 17th November, landing at Boulogne. At first they were concentrated near Morbecque. By April 1916 they had been transferred to the 86th Brigade, 29th Division on the 25th of April. They fought on the first day of the Battle of the Somme attacking Hawthorne Ridge and were decimated losing 24 officers and 500 other ranks in the attack. There followed a period of reorganisation as fresh troops were transferred to them to bring them up to strength. On 8th October the 16th Battalion were sent once to the Somme area and were moved to the neighbourhood of Mametz Wood on 13th October. They remained in this area until Sir Douglas Haig finally called a halt to the Battle on 18th November 1916. On the 21st November the 16th Battalion were sent to man the trenches near Lesboeufs, north of Morval. Here, three days later on *24th November 1916* William was killed aged 29. He is buried in the A.I.F. Burial Ground, Flers.

Chapter 5

1917

1917 was another year which started with hope. In Britain a Coalition Government had been formed with Lloyd George as Prime Minister. In France General Robert Nivelle had replaced Marshal Joseph Joffre as the commander of the French armies on the Western Front in December 1916. Nivelle claimed that a massive barrage on German lines would bring France victory in 48 hours. It was hoped that the slaughter of the kind seen on the Somme would be at an end with Nivelle's belief that the hoped for breakthrough would at last be achieved. On the other fronts 1917 would see Russia face two revolutions in March and November. The latter would take them out of the war. The loss of Russia was partly offset by the USA joining the war against the Central Powers in April. Unfortunately Nivelle's plans ended in tatters as the fighting once more descended into carnage.

29. Captain James Neilson Greenlees Stafford – 6th Battalion Royal Warwickshire Regiment. He was the second son of Thomas and Elizabeth Stafford of Bristol Road, Edgbaston. He was educated at West House School and then at Tonbridge School. He excelled at sport and was a regular member of the Moseley pack for some years and frequently played for the Midland Counties in the inter-county championship matches. He was described by one commentator as 'the speediest forward' he had ever seen. He was also acting as secretary at *Moseley Rugby Club* before the outbreak of war. He was a member of Birmingham Rowing Club and had at one time won the championship at the club. He was a member of the firm of Messrs. Edward Stone, Hooper and Pickard, auctioneers and estate agents, Birmingham. In 1911 he was living at Charford Vesey Road, Wylde Green, Birmingham.

On the outbreak of war he was granted a commission in the 6th Battalion Royal Warwickshire Regiment, one of the local Territorial Battalions. At the start of the war the battalion was stationed in Birmingham and later moved to Chelmsford as part of the South Midland Division. On the 22nd March 1915 they were mobilised for war and landed at Havre as part of the 143rd Brigade of the 48th Division. Their first major action was the Battle of the Somme on 1st July 1916. Their target was the Heidenkopf Quadrilateral. During the fighting James was shot through the left wrist but despite this he continued to lead his men forward until he collapsed through loss of blood. He was sent back to England for treatment and eventually ended up at the First Southern General Hospital at Birmingham University. James was promoted to captain on his return to the Battalion. In February 1917 Germans had strengthened their positions by retreating to a newly prepared and formidable new line of defence known as the Hindenburg Line. The Division occupied the Peronne region during this retreat thus sparing them from the Battle of Arras taking place further north. Despite this there was still fighting in their region and James was killed on *16th April 1917*, aged 28, leading his men to the enemy lines. He is buried in the Saulcourt Churchyard Extension, Guyencourt-Saulcourt.

30. Lieutenant Alistair MacNiven – 7th Battalion Cameron Highlanders. He was the son of William and Annie MacNiven, of 19 Oakland Road, Moseley, Birmingham. In 1911 he was a Law Student and later became a solicitor. He played football for *Moor Green Football Club.*

He enlisted in the 7th Battalion Cameron Highlanders in September 1914 because of his family's Scottish connections. The Battalion became part of the 44th Brigade, 15th (Scottish) Division. In March 1915 he was promoted to 2nd Lieutenant. The Battalion moved to France on 9th July 1915 and saw action in the Battle of Loos, 25th September to 8th October 1915. Then during 1916 they fought in the Battle of the Somme. Alistair was twice wounded and was promoted to Lieutenant. In April 1917, the Battalion was involved in the Second Battle of Arras, moving out of billets at Arras and relieving the 8th /10th Gordon Highlanders in the Front Line trenches on Sunday 22nd April ready for an attack on Guémappe. They attacked in darkness in the early hours of the morning of 23rd April. Immediately they were met with a counter barrage and withering machine gun fire from the Germans. Despite this the German front line trenches were reached and the attack moved on and then dug in facing strong German counterattacks. When they were eventually pulled back to their own lines it was found that the battalion had nearly half its officers as casualties with 4 killed and 369 casualties from other ranks out of 570 with 79 killed. Alistair was severely wounded in the fighting and taken back to Duisans Casualty Clearing Station where he died on 23rd April 1917 aged 27. He was buried on *1st May 1917* at the Duisans British Cemetery, Etrun.

31. Captain John Chamberlain – 3rd Battalion South Wales Borderers, 14th Battalion Welsh Regiment. Military Cross. He was born on 22nd December 1881, and was the younger son of Arthur Chamberlain JP of Moor Green Hall, Moor Green Lane, Moseley, Birmingham. His father was a younger brother of Joseph Chamberlain and had taken over the business interests of the latter in 1900. He was chairman of Kynoch Ltd, Birmingham,  manufacturers of explosives and small arms ammunition. John was educated at Rugby (1895-1899) and read Engineering and Electrical Engineering at Birmingham University, which he entered in the year of its foundation in 1900. He won the 220 yards handicap in the University Sports in 1902, but his principal sport was Rugby, in which he represented his school, his University, *Moseley Rugby Club* and the Midland Counties. In 1903 John took over the management of Chamberlain & Hookham from his father. He also became a director of Thomas Smith Stamping Works, Credenda Conduits, and Tubes (Limited). He took an interest in local affairs, becoming a JP in Birmingham in 1909. He married Hilda Poynting, the younger daughter of J F Poynting, Professor of Physics at Birmingham University and went on to have a son and three daughters. They lived at Beechcroft, Westbourne Road, Edgbaston.

John could have been exempted from war service because of the important industrial positions that he held but instead enlisted in the 6th Battalion Royal Warwickshire Regiment on 9th September 1914, the same Battalion as his fellow Moseley teammate James Stafford. He was commissioned as a 2nd Lieutenant in the 3rd Battalion South Wales Borderers on 6th October 1914.

Again he could have remained in this country and, due to his management experience, was employed in army administration to begin with, however he opted to serve in France. He was transferred to the 1st Battalion Welsh Regiment and saw action in the Second Battle of Ypres in April 1915. He was wounded in the stomach whilst throwing bombs at the Germans and spent some time in hospital in England. During this period he was promoted to Lieutenant. He returned to the front and was promoted Captain on 1st October 1915. He was Acting Staff Captain of the 15th Battalion Welsh Regiment during the Battle of the Somme in 1916. During his military service he was offered a government post on three occasions but declined each time. In April 1917 he returned to the Front as second in command of the 14th Battalion Welsh Regiment. On *14th May 1917*, while in temporary command of the battalion, John was killed by a stray shell at Boesinghe in the Ypres salient and was posthumously awarded the Military Cross. He is buried in Grave 2, Row B, Plot 2 in Fermier-Olivier Cemetery, Elverdinghe, Ypres.

32. Private Edward O'Brien – 545763 2nd London Sanitary Company. He (Teddy) was born in Bournville, Birmingham and was the son of the late Thomas O'Brien and husband of Elsie Sarah Winckle (formerly O'Brien), of Needwood, Streetsbrook Road, Solihull, Birmingham. He was Secretary of *Ashfield Cricket Club* from 1902-1911 and was an efficient umpire. He also played football for *Moor Green Football Club*. He died aged 36, from an affection of the heart, due to the strain of military duties on *14th August 1917* and is buried in Handsworth Cemetery, Birmingham.

33. Lieutenant (Edmund) Kenneth Wallace Brown 3rd/5th or 6th Battalion Royal Warwickshire Regiment. Kenneth Brown (only one from Birmingham on the Hall of Memory site and he is listed as K Brown although just to add confusion his first name was Edmund!) The Commonwealth War Graves Commission site has him in the 6th Battalion but the men are recorded as the 5th and the commanding officer was in charge of 3rd/5th. He was born in 1893 in Brownhills and was the son of Dr D.W. Brown formerly Mayor of Preston. In 1911 he was 17 years of age and was an insurance clerk at the Royal Exchange. He was living with his sister Gertrude Helen Brown, aged 36 at 16 Moseley Road, Moseley. She was a secondary school teacher at King Edward's Grammar School, Birmingham. He played rugby for *Moseley Rugby Club*.

He went to France with probably the 6th Battalion Royal Warwickshire Regiment on 16th July 1917. He was injured on the Somme and was sent home for treatment and then joined the 3rd/5th Battalion Royal Warwickshire Regiment. This was a home based reserved battalion. His death was one of great bravery. On the morning of Friday 24th August 1917, Lieutenant Colonel Frank Martin Chatterley and over 600 of his men, including Kenneth, set off on a route march from their camp to the nearby town of Blyth on the Northumberland coast, just a few miles away. It was a hot day, and Colonel Chatterley called a halt at the beach for 20 minutes to allow the men to bathe and cool off. As there were several hundred of them, they took up most of the beach between the West Pier and the Link House. Hot and sweaty in their serge uniforms, it was not long before the young soldiers had stripped off and rushed into the inviting water. None of them were aware that the tide was ebbing, and that in that part of the bay a number of deep channels cut into the sand by the currents caused the water to rush out with irresistible force. On that particular day there was a strong westerly wind, and a strong sea running.

Within minutes some of the men of Kenneth's Company appeared to be in difficulty and shouted for help. Further out than the rest, they appeared to be swimming frantically against strong currents, but making no headway and being taken out to sea. There was an immediate response from the shore as men who considered themselves strong swimmers went to help their colleagues. These men, too, got into difficulties, and in a short time there were about 15 battling hopelessly against the currents. Kenneth quickly organised the men into lines and, joining hands, they waded out to try and rescue the now drowning soldiers. The Chaplain, Captain Verschoyle, did likewise and between them, and with the assistance of Sergeant John Riley, they managed to get seven of the men out of the water. Three of the rescued men were completely exhausted, if not unconscious, and were immediately put into vehicles and taken from the beach. The undercurrent was so strong that it was almost impossible even to wade, and in trying to reach another of his men Kenneth was swept off his feet. He clung on to the man next to him but, unable to retain his grip, was swept away by the swirling water. Captain Verschoyle tried desperately save him, but in vain, and found himself in severe difficulties. He was dragged from the sea, gasping for breath and utterly exhausted. There were no boats immediately available, either in the bay itself or on the shore. After the alarm was raised, the Harbour Commissioner's steam launch, the Waterwitch, and other boats came to the scene, but they were too late to save any of the men.

In all, nine men including Kenneth lost their lives. Sergeant John Riley (25) was due to be married the following day, having just returned from 18 months at the front, and his clothes and rail warrant were ready in his room for him to catch the train that evening. The other seven were all very young soldiers: Private George Beavan (18), Private Jesse Blunn (17), Private Thomas Forley (18), Private William Henderson (18), Private Gordon Moy (18), Private Fred Shale (18) and Private Henry Southern (18). Later that day, teams from the Royal Navy searched the area with boats and, using lifelines held by others on the shore, managed to recover six of the bodies. Unfortunately, those of Kenneth, Jesse Blunn and William Henderson were not among them. Over the course of the next few days, two of the three bodies were found, although Kenneth's was not recovered until 6th September 1917, when it was discovered close to the Link House by John Dent, a Gunner in the Royal Artillery. The Coroner for the area, Mr Henry Rutherford, held an inquest into the tragedy. It was not the first time people had drowned in the bay, and he made some strong recommendations. In future, he said, officers contemplating sending their men bathing at Blythe should seek local advice as to the state of the tide and the currents. He also noted that many of the soldiers could not swim, and many had not even seen the sea before. Kenneth Brown's attempts to save his men, and his subsequent inability to retain his grip, were probably explained by the fact that he had been seriously wounded at the Quadrilateral on the First Day of the Somme. He was hit by a bullet just above his right elbow, which then fractured. Although the exit and entry wounds healed, he was left with limited movement in his right arm. It was brave of him even to try to rescue his men in his condition. He died aged 23 on *24th August 1917* and is buried in the Horton (St. Mary) Churchyard, Blyth Cemetery.

34. Lieutenant George Elliot Austin – 6th Battalion Royal Warwickshire Regiment. He was born on 17th November 1892 in Whitchurch in Shropshire the youngest son of William and Kate Austin. He was educated at the Royal Masonic School, Bushey 1901-1910. He played hockey for Hertfordshire and cricket for *Ashfield Cricket Club*. In 1911 he was aged 18 and was living at 1 Oliver Road, Oakland Road, Moseley, Birmingham, as a border. He was an insurance clerk at the Alliance Assurance Company, Birmingham.

George enlisted as Private in the Territorials before 1914 and went to France on 22nd March 1915. He was promoted to Sergeant and then obtained a commission. The 6th Battalion were involved in the Third Battle of Ypres which began on 31st July and continued until 10th November 1917. The battle took place, for control of the ridges south and east of the Belgian city of Ypres in West Flanders. Passchendaele lay on the last ridge east of Ypres, 5 miles from a railway junction at Roulers, which was vital to the supply system of the German 4th Army. The next stage of the Allied plan was an advance to Thourout-Couckelaere, to close the German-controlled railway running through Roulers and Thourout. The British also hoped to turn northwards towards Bruge and capture the submarine bases which were causing havoc on the shipping heading for Britain and causing food shortages. Haig also felt that the attack was needed because of the perilous state of the French Army which had suffered mutinies since the failure of the Nivelle Offensive earlier in the year. The battle met initial success but then struggled to make significant progress as rain began to fall. By 18th August when the Battle of Langemarck came to an end there had been four main battles but the Germans continued to hold the high ground and inflict heavy casualties on the advancing troop. From the 19th August a series of local attacks took place and began to make small but significant gains. Unfortunately the weather continued to worsen. The night of 26th/27th August was one of heavy rain and intense darkness. The following morning, 27th August brought further downpours making the state of the ground even worse than before. The great bog of shell-holes had become almost impassable. II Corps tried a combined tank and infantry attack but the tanks bogged, the attack failed and Haig called a halt to operations until the weather improved. During this attack George was killed by a machine gun bullet while leading C Company in an attack. He died on *27th August 1917*. His body was not found and he is remembered on the Tyne Cot Memorial.

35. Lieutenant Hugh Randolph Ryan-Bell – 1st/8th Battalion Worcestershire Regiment. He was the eldest son of John and Annie Ryan-Bell and the husband of Maude Marie Ryan-Bell, of "Graiseley", Wheelwright Road, Erdington, Birmingham. He was born in Moseley, Birmingham and attended King Edward's School. He was manager of the Sparkbrook Branch of Lloyds Bank. He was a well-known member of *Ashfield*

Cricket Club and Kings Norton Golf Club. He had been married for nine months.

When the war began he joined the 14th Battalion (1st Birmingham Pals) Royal Warwickshire Regiment as private 14/487. He was promoted to 2nd Lieutenant and then Lieutenant in the 1st/8th Battalion Worcestershire Regiment in August 1915. During 1916 the Battalion fought in the Battle of the Somme. Then in July 1917 they fought in the Third Battle of Ypres. In the same attack as George Austin, Hugh led his men forward in the attack on Springfield Farm. Whilst doing so he was shot by rifle fire. He continued to fight but was then hit again by a shell burst. He was taken to a Clearing Station and then to a Base Hospital for treatment but died of his wounds aged 30 on *29th August 1917*. The Captain of his company wrote that the attack on Springfield Farm '…was not in our line but the Battalion that attacked it was repulsed. Seeing this Colonel Carr ordered an attack by D Company, which by this time was almost level with the house… This brilliant attack was commanded by Captain Ryan Bell, who was mortally wounded. Had he lived he would have received the DSO.' He is buried in the Dozinghem Military Cemetery.

36. 2nd Lieutenant Harry Raymond Rawlinson – 7th Battalion Worcestershire, 1st/8th Battalion Machine Gun Corps (Infantry). He was born in Caistor, Lincolnshire 1893 to Alfred and Emma Rawlinson, of Market Place, Market Rasen, Lincolnshire. He was a bank clerk in Dudley in 1911 but was working at Lloyds Bank in Birmingham when he enlisted in September 1914. He played football for *Moor Green Football Club*.

He joined the 7th Worcestershire Regiment in 1914 and rose to the rank of sergeant after taking a machine gun course. He went to France in March 1916 and fought in the Battle of the Somme. He returned to England in November 1916 and was commissioned in the Machine Gun Corps. In 1917 he fought in the Third Battle of Ypres. On 26th September 1917, after a pause for the dreadful weather, the second phase of the battle began with the Battle of Polygon Wood. This took place from the Menin Road to Polygon Wood and then north, to the area beyond St. Julien. The plan was a much smaller advance to take place covering 1,000-1,500 yards and stopping on the reverse slopes of the high ground which were easier to defend and would also have observation of German reinforcement routes and counter-attack assembly areas. The attack was a success with significant gains made by the British when it closed on 7th October. Unfortunately Harry was amongst the many casualties of the battle dying, aged 23, on *26th September 1917* and is buried in the Hooge Crater Cemetery.

37. Private Frederic Howard Inns – 10573 2nd Battalion Honourable Artillery Company. He was the son of Frederic and Annie Inns, of 6, Ashfield Road, Kings Heath, Birmingham and husband of Jessica Inns. In 1911 he was a commercial traveller in jewellery and was living in a cottage in Coldbank Lane, Hall Green and later at 7 Clarence Road, Moseley. He married Jessica in 1910. He played cricket for *Ashfield Cricket Club*.

He was in the Reserves and was posted to France on 7th March 1917. Almost immediately he was involved in the Third Battle of Ypres. He fought in the Battle of Poelcappelle on 9th October 1917. This was the fourth of a series of "bite and hold" battles launched by General Herbert Plumer and each achieved their objectives, biting chunks out of the German line and then defending those gains against any counter-attacks. Each of the attacks had been supported by a well-directed artillery bombardment that had isolated the part of the German front line as well as by a creeping barrage that had protected the advancing soldiers. Unfortunately on the 7th October it began to rain again and continued for the next two days and so, when the battle began on the 9th October, the ground was saturated making movement difficult and the bombardment was less successful with less stable platforms and many shells ineffectually falling in the mud. By contrast the German artillery had much more stable platforms and were directed against the advancing troops and the British artillery. The result was that the Battle of Poelcappelle failed to achieve its objectives and Frederic was amongst those killed. He died aged 34 on *9th October 1917* and is remembered on Tyne Cot Memorial.

38. Lieutenant William James Pearce – 2nd/5th Battalion Gloucestershire Regiment. He was the son of James Pearce, of Linton, Gloucester and husband of Margery Barrett (formerly Pearce), of 34, Wellington Road, Bilston, Staffordshire and later 88 Leyland Road, Southport, Lancashire. He was vice-captain of *Moseley Rugby Club*.

On the outbreak of war he joined the 1st/5th Battalion South Staffordshire Regiment as a Lance Sergeant (2963). He went to France with them on 5th

March 1915. When he got his commission he was transferred to the 2nd/5th Battalion Gloucestershire Regiment. The 2nd/5th Gloucestershire was a second line Territorial battalion, formed in Gloucester in September 1914 and allocated to the 2nd/1st Gloucester & Worcester Brigade of the 2nd South Midland Division. In August 1915 they joined the 184th Brigade, 61st Division. The battalion began its active service in the Laventie sector where the newly arrived division was alongside the newly arrived 5th Australian Division. Both divisions took part in the ill-fated attack on Fromelles in July which cost the Australians 5,500 casualties and the 61st Division 1,550. The battalion moved down to the Somme at the end of October, too late for any of the battles but in time to follow up the German retreat to the Hindenburg Line in March/April 1917. Later in the year they were involved in the Third Battle Ypres and then, from 20th November to 7th December 1917, the Battle of Cambrai. This was the first big tank battle and brought a great deal of success for the Allied forces on the first day and then, as many of the tanks experienced mechanical difficulties and the Germans regrouped, the progress again began to stall. The Germans began a massive counter-attack employing the new tactics of a short, intense period of shelling followed by a rapid assault. During one of these counter-attacks William was killed. He died aged 33 on *2nd December 1917* and is buried in the Villers-Plouich Communal Cemetery.

39. Captain Roland Bevington Gibbins – 2nd/8th Battalion Royal Warwickshire Regiment. He was the youngest son of Richard Cadbury Gibbons and Caroline Gibbins, of 'Fayreslowe' 62, Wellington Road, Edgbaston, Birmingham. He was the husband of Edith Grace Gibbins, of 20, Pakenham Road, Edgbaston, Birmingham. They married in 1916. He was born on 19th October 1885. He was educated at Sedbergh and then at King's College Cambridge where he took he took his Degree with honours in the Natural Sciences Tripos in 1907. He played rugby at Cambridge against Oxford in 1905 and 1906 and was on the winning side both times. He then played for *Moseley Rugby Club*. The *Moseley and Kings Heath Journal* records him as '…a conspicuous player in the pack… There is little doubt that with further opportunities of playing he would have gained his international cap.' He represented the Midland Counties in the Rugby Union Championship.

In 1906 he was chosen for the international trial match and represented the south against the north at Blackheath. He also played for Cambridge University. There is little doubt that with further opportunities of playing he would have gained his international cap. He was a director of J. and E. Sturge Limited, chemical manufacturers and he was also a member of the Society of Friends.

He joined the 28th Battalion London Regiment (Artists' Rifles) and was Lance Corporal (4816) in the latter part of 1915. The Artists' Rifles had gone to France in October 1914 and had become an Officers Training Corps. Roland received his commission in the 2nd /8th Battalion Royal Warwickshire Regiment in 7th July 1916 and was then promoted to Captain. The 2nd/8th Royal Warwickshire Regiment was in the 182nd Brigade, 61st (2nd South Midland) Division, which was the same as his friend William Pearce. He died on the same day, *3rd December 1917* aged 32, and is remembered on the Cambrai Memorial, Louverval.

40. Captain Leysters Llewellyn Greener *Military Cross* – 2nd/6th Battalion Royal Warwickshire Regiment. On the Moseley Memorial he is listed as W. Greener. There is one possibility from Birmingham, and for a time I thought it was him, but Leysters is far more likely. He was the son of Charles and Harriet Greener of "The Rookery", Hartopp Road, Four Oaks, Sutton Coldfield.

He was the grandson of W.W. Greener, founder of Birmingham Gun Makers. He was educated at Rugby School where he was in the Officer's Training Corps and was captain of the football fifteen and the shooting eight. He was also a member of the gymnasium team. He joined the Territorial Force about 18 months before the outbreak of war, receiving his commission in the 6th Royal Warwickshire Regiment in February 1913. I could find no reference to him playing for *Moseley Rugby Club* but with the Rugby School connection I cannot imagine Moseley letting him slip through.

He joined the 1st/6th Battalion Royal Warwickshire Regiment. He went to France with them on 22nd March 1915. He won the Military Cross in June 1915 when he led his men to the edge of a recently created crater and held off the Germans whilst trenches were dug to the crater. He lost his right eye in September 1915 during a grenade throwing exercise when a fuse went off in his hand. He was eventually sent to England for further treatment. He was promoted to Lieutenant in late October 1915 and Temporary Captain in September 1916 before being promoted to Captain in June 1917. By then he was in the 2nd/6th Royal Warwickshire Regiment. On 5th December 1917, during the Battle of Cambrai, he was killed in a bombing duel with the Germans. His commanding officer said that he would have recommended him for the DSO had he lived. He died aged 24 on *5th December 1917* and is remembered on the Cambrai Memorial, Louverval.

Chapter 6

1918-1921

The beginning of the year was in sharp contrast to the beginning of 1917 where the year had been welcomed with hope and optimism. The losses of Arras and Passchendaele as well as the loss of Russia, which had only been partly offset by the entry of the USA, and food shortages meant that people face the new year with resolution but with little hope that the year would see the end of the nightmare of war. The Russians would eventually officially leave the war with the Treaty of Brest-Litovsk in March 1918 but were no longer fighting on the Eastern Front. This meant that Germany had extra troops to hurl at the Western Front before the forces of the USA could become involved. On 21st March 1918 the Germans launched their Spring Offensive and for a time it looked as if they might finally win the war causing heavy allied losses and making substantial gains in territory but overstretched supply lines and heavy casualties amongst their irreplaceable elite troops meant that they were susceptible to an Allied counter-attack. Their offensive was halted in July 1918 and then the Allies went on the offensive and the Germans were gradually forced backwards. Both sides suffered heavy casualties but it was the end for Germany. Her allies surrendered one by one and then, in November 1918, revolts occurred in various parts of the country causing the Kaiser to abdicate. On 11th November 1918 the Armistice was signed bringing to an end the fighting on the Western Front.

41. 2nd Lieutenant Gerald Edward Drake – 10th Battalion Worcestershire Regiment. He was born in 1881 in Banbury, the son of Edward and Susan Drake. His father was a commercial traveller. He had a sister Marjorie Helen Benedicta Drake (born 1883). He was educated at Chigwell School. In 1900 he was admitted to Trinity Hall, Cambridge University in 1900 and received his BA in 1903. He was a schoolmaster at Green Hall School, Belper 1902-1903 and at Royal School, Armagh, Ireland (1903-1907). He was a member of *Moseley Golf Club*.

At the outbreak of war he joined the 10th Battalion Worcestershire Regiment as Private 33950. He was later commissioned in the same regiment. The 10th Battalion was formed at Worcester in September 1914 as part of Kitchener's New Armies, and came under orders of 57th Brigade in 19th (Western) Division. They landed in France on 18th July 1915 and fought in many of the major battles of 1916 and 1917. At the end of 1917 they had seen action at Welsh Ridge. There were no major engagements in January 1918 and so we can conclude that Gerald died from shell fire, a trench raid or sniping. He died on *26th January 1918* and is buried in the Neuville-Bourjonval British Cemetery.

42. Private Frederick Arthur Woodcock – 286 'B' Company 5 Platoon 14th Battalion (1st Birmingham Pals) Royal Warwickshire Regiment. He was the only child of Arthur Woodcock, of 130, Colmore Row, Birmingham, and the Annie Harriet Woodcock (Ebdy) and was born in Sheffield. He was an ex-pupil of King Edward's School, Camp Hill, Birmingham and excelled at football and cricket but his love was rowing. He was the secretary of the Birmingham Rowing Club. He also  played football for *Moor Green Football Club*. He was employed at the Aston Road Branch of Lloyds Bank. In 1911 the family were living at 10 Bloomfield Road, Moseley.

On the outbreak of war he joined the 14th Battalion (1st Birmingham Pals) Royal Warwickshire Regiment. He went to France on the 14th November 1915. The Battalion saw action in the Battle of the Somme where they suffered many casualties. They also fought in battles throughout 1917 including the Third Battle of Ypres. Frederick survived all these battles but the strain of fighting, and possible gassing, weakened him considerably and he was invalided home with what was diagnosed as a heart defect in December 1918. He was treated at the Fir Vale Hospital in Sheffield but died of sickness, aged 34, on *3rd February 1918* and is buried in Brandwood Cemetery, Birmingham.

43. Captain Walter Reynolds Mansell – 5th Battalion South Staffordshire Regiment. He was born on 14th January 1892 and was the son of Charles and Charlotte Mansell of 26 Park Road, Moseley, Birmingham (formerly of Wentworth Road, Harborne and later at 58, Calthorpe Road, Edgbaston.) His father was a tyre merchant. He was educated at King Edward's School where he was a keen sportsman at rugby and athletics. Prior to the war he was employed by the Clipper Tyre Company Limited. He played rugby for *Moseley Rugby Club* where he was a skilful three-quarter with a wonderful dodge. He was also a member of the Garden and Priory Tennis clubs.

In 1914, Walter enlisted as a Private Soldier in the 2nd Birmingham Pals Battalion 15th Royal Warwickshire Regiment, and reached the rank of Corporal. On 4th July 1915 he was promoted to 2nd Lieutenant to the South Staffordshire Regiment, serving as a Musketry Officer. He was sent to France in July 1916, and transferred to the 5th Battalion as a Lieutenant, serving as a Bombing Officer. In September of that year, he was wounded and invalided home, suffering from trench fever and severe influenza. He re-joined the 5th Battalion in October 1917. In December 1917, following another wound, Walter was promoted to Acting Captain, and went on to suffer a severe wound at St Quentin on *24th March 1918*, subsequently dying of his wounds at the 3rd Canadian Hospital, Étaples, on 16th April 1918. He is buried in Étaples Military Cemetery, France.

44. Gunner Wilfred Leslie Hales – 163139 280th Siege Battery Royal Garrison Artillery. He was the son of Mr Edward and Mary Hales, of 254, Kingsbury Road, Erdington, Birmingham and husband of Brenda F. Hales, of 4, Waterloo Terrace, Newhampton Road, Wolverhampton. He was born in Solihull in 1886. He played football for *Moor Green Football Club*. In 1911 he was single and was working as a bank clerk. He lived at 244 Kingsbury Road, Erdington. He married Brenda Sichel in Bideford in 1915.

He enlisted in the 280th Siege Battery Royal Garrison Artillery. Siege Batteries, Royal Garrison Artillery were equipped with heavy howitzers, sending large calibre high explosive shells in high trajectory, plunging fire. The usual armaments were 6 inch, 8 inch and 9.2 inch howitzers, although some had huge railway- or road-mounted 12 inch howitzers. As British artillery tactics developed, the Siege Batteries were most often employed in destroying or neutralising the enemy artillery, as well as putting destructive fire down on strongpoints, dumps, store, roads and railways behind enemy lines. Wilfred died of pneumonia on *24th April 1918* aged 32 and is buried in Saint Marie Cemetery, Le Havre.

45. Private Herbert Leslie Tomlinson 835572 "C" Battery 58th Brigade Royal Field Artillery. On the war memorial the name is listed as P.L. Tomlinson but again this is wrong. He was the son of Henry and Janet Tomlinson, of 12, Amesbury Road, Moseley, Birmingham and was born in 1896. In September 1907 Herbert was admitted to King Edward's School. When he left school in 1912 he went to work for Wolseley Motors Limited, Adderley Park, Birmingham. He played football for *Moor Green Football Club*.

At the outbreak of war in 1914, Herbert enlisted with the Royal Engineers as a Despatch Rider and later was promoted to Corporal. He was then transferred into the Royal Field Artillery (Gunner 5964). He went to France on 1st April 1915 and was twice gassed and wounded. In early 1918, the brigade was stationed north of Lens near the town of Mazingarbe. This was fortunate for them since they happened to be in the part of the line which was not subject to the German Spring Offensives from March till June 1918. Unfortunately on the night of 22nd May 1918 he had the misfortune of being at the No.10 Stationary Hospital in St. Omer. That night the Germans dropped three bombs on the hospital virtually destroying the hospital but miraculously the number of casualties were small taking into account the amount of damage done. None of the nursing staff were hurt but a Territorial officer, Major Elliott and another medical officer had been killed. Unfortunately Herbert was buried under the rubble and he was posted as missing. Only later was his body found. He died aged 22 on *22nd May 1918*. He was buried at Longuenesse (St Omer) Souvenir Cemetery. He was just twenty-one years old.

46. Captain Charles Leslie Young – Royal Air Force – (The Ashfield Memorial records an L. Young. The Birmingham Hall of Memory site does not record any Youngs. When Charles died his death notice records his father as coming from Moseley and so this entry seems the most plausible explanation.) He was born in Balsall Heath, Birmingham on 28th June 1891 to Charles and Maud Young. He was the youngest of three children and their only son. In 1911 he was living on the Balsall Heath Road and was in charge of the English export department of Messrs Wills and Son (tobacco merchants) in Birmingham. He played football for *Moor Green Football Club*.

When he enlisted he joined the Royal Naval Air Service. In 1917 he passed his flying exam in an Avro Biplane at the Royal Naval Air Station at Redcar. He was living at 131 Linden Road, Handsworth, Birmingham. He was awarded the Distinguished Service Cross in 1917 after action against a German submarine. He died aged 26 on *30th May 1918* and is remembered on the Hollybrook Memorial, Southampton, as he was lost at sea. He was killed whilst flying a Curtis H-12, 8660 of RAF Great Yarmouth, on long reconnaissance patrol to the Borkhum area. The plane was forced to land on the sea due to engine trouble. The crew of the plane were Captain Charles Leslie Young DSC, Ensign George Thomas Roe USNFC, Corporal Grant 211338, Private W.S. Chase 213914 and Private Jack W. Money. His gravestone in Warstone Lane Cemetery Birmingham, records that he was killed "… on the North Sea by the Germans whilst his seaplane was lying helpless on the water owing to engine trouble." This is confirmed by a website which records that his aircraft was "attacked by enemy seaplanes when boat alighted due to engine trouble." Charles Young was killed with at least two others of the crew whilst the remainder were taken prisoner.

47. Private Alfred Blackham 74526 Royal Army Medical Corps attached to 384th Siege Battery Royal Garrison Artillery. He was the eldest son of F.B. and Mary Emma Blackham, of 57, Jakeman Road, Balsall Heath, Birmingham. He was one of six brothers who served. (On the Ashfield War Memorial he is listed as F.B. Blackham. There are 3 Blackmans on the Hall of Memory site: A, E.T. and H. Alfred lived in Amesbury Road, Moseley but I can't see how he could be F.B. and Edward Thomas is also a possibility as he lived in Woodlands Road. My speculation is that they used the father's initials by mistake.) He played football for *Moor Green Football Club*.

The 384th Siege Battery joined the 13th (Western) Division in Mesopotamia on 25th October 1917. They were in action during the Second and Third Actions of Jabril Hamrin and fought at Tuz Khurmatli the following April. By 28th May 1918 they had moved to Dhawlib enduring extreme summer temperatures. He died aged 34 on *21st June 1918* and is remembered on the Basra Memorial.

48. Walter Hughes of *Moseley Golf Club* has defeated me. There are just too many possibilities for W. Hughes with a Birmingham connection. This one is pure speculation but at least fits in with the other members of *Moseley Golf Club*. *Captain Charles Walter Hughes* 14th Battalion (1st Birmingham Pals) Royal Warwickshire Regiment. He was the son of James and Annie Elizabeth Hughes. He lived in Woodbridge Road, Moseley. He worked for Messrs Bass & Co in Hill Street, Belfast before he moved to Birmingham.

In September 1914 he enlisted in the 14th Battalion Royal Warwickshire Regiment with the number 302 and was commissioned on the 4th February 1915. He was promoted to the rank of Captain on 17th June 1917. Between 4th and 13th September 1918 the 14th Battalion were bivouacked near the village of Sapignies. During their next period of engagement they were in action against the formidable Hindenburg Line against a section known as the African Trench. The attack had begun on the 27th September and was to last three days with the Hindenburg Line finally being breached but with heavy casualties from the British forces. Captain Charles Walter Hughes was 38 when he died of wounds on *1st October 1918* after being shot through the head as he stood on a parapet at the head of his Company.

49. 2nd Lieutenant Stanley Phillips Fryer – 30th Brigade Royal Field Artillery. He was the son of Herbert and Edith Maud Fryer, of Swansea and was the husband of Bertha Mary Fryer, of 15, George Street, Balsall Heath, Birmingham. In 1911 he was 25 and married. He was a commercial traveller for blue starch, black lead and metal polish. He was living at 33 Featherstone Road. He was born in Swansea. He played football for *Moor Green Football Club*.

He joined the Honourable Artillery and went to Egypt on 12th November 1915. Both A and B Batteries of the Honourable Artillery Company went to Suez in April 1915. In July, B Battery fought in the recapture of Sheikh Othman. In February 1917, both batteries took part in the Palestine Campaign, were in action at the First and Second Battle of Gaza and entered Jerusalem in December 1917. On 23rd February 1918 he was commissioned in the Royal Field Artillery. He died on *27th October 1918* aged 33 and is buried in La Vallee-Mulatre Communal Cemetery Extension.

50. Captain Hugh Lancelot Evers Military Cross and Bar – 2nd/8th Battalion Worcestershire Regiment. He was the sixth and youngest son of Frank and Isabel Evers, of White Hall, Stourbridge. He attended King Edward

VI Grammar School Stourbridge from 1893-94. After this he went to Birmingham University and studied chemistry and metallurgy. He went to work at the Round Oak Steel Works near Dudley and later worked in Worcester as a partner in the Industrial Foundry and Engineering Company Limited. As a young man he was a keen rugby player for *Moseley Rugby Club* where he was a formidable forward.

When war broke out in August 1914 he joined the 2nd/8th Battalion Worcester Regiment as Private 2778 and was then commissioned in November 1914 in the same Battalion. They were deployed to France in May 1916 as part of the 61st Division. The battalion was in action on the Somme in 1916 and in the advance to the Hindenburg Line in 1917. By the Third Battle of Ypres (31st July 1917) he had been promoted to Acting Captain and in charge of a Company. The Battle of Langemarck (16th-18th August) was the second major attack during the Third Battle of Ypres. It ended because of the wet weather. After it ended there were a series of local attacks with small gains been made with heavy losses but again the very wet weather and the cloying mud held up the British advance. The 2nd/8th Battalion were involved in the last of these attacks on 27th August when the II Corps tried a combined tank and infantry attack. The 2nd/8th Battalion attacked around Aisne Farm. They moved from water-filled shell hole to shell hole, all the time being pinned down by withering machine gun fire and a ferocious barrage. Rifles became clogged with mud and the wounded sank back into the shell holes to drown in the slimy ponds. The tanks soon became bogged down and eventually Haig halted the attack until the weather improved. As a result of Evers actions at this time, he was later awarded the Military Cross on 18th October 1917 'For conspicuous gallantry and devotion to duty'. His citation stated that 'Although severely wounded at the commencement of an attack, he continued to command his company for three hours, and didn't have his wound attended until he had seen his company established in their position after the attack.'

Evers went to a hospital at Le Treport before being sent back to England in September 1917 where he attended the First Southern General Hospital in Birmingham. By December he had been transferred to an auxiliary hospital near Shrewsbury where he stayed until May 1918. In the middle of May he was passed fit to return to his Battalion and eventually returned to the front in June 1918. From September 1918 the 2nd/8th Battalion was involved in the Hundred Days Offensive from 18th July to the Armistice on 11th November 1918. On the 3rd September Evers achieved a second Military Cross and added a Bar to his first cross. The citation said that this occurred whilst his Battalion was engaged in the crossing of the River Lys east of Estaires. He acted with great courage and inspiring confidence as he twice led his men in outflanking attacks on enemy machine gun positions, capturing both. The offensive continued throughout September and October. On 24th October a barrage preceded another offensive but the Germans continued to resist tenaciously and inflict casualties on the Allies. On 30th October the 2nd/8th Battalion became involved in the offensive at Mareches. On *1st November 1918* Captain Lancelot Evers was killed, aged 37, as his Battalion advanced. He is buried in the Crucifix Cemetery, Vendegies-Sur-Ecaillon.

And so the war deaths on the memorials come to an end but that isn't the end of the story for the Ashfield Memorial records two further deaths. The last is obviously a result of war the former less obvious.

51. Captain *Sydney Graham Halsey* 9th Battalion Cheshire Regiment. His parents lived at 9 Oxford Road, Moseley, Birmingham but his medal card records his address as Hurst Pierrepoint College, Sussex. He was born in Gloucester in 1891. He was an assistant manager of a public company. He played cricket for *Ashfield Cricket Club* and football for *Moor Green Football Club*. He was sent to France on 19th July 1915 and served throughout the war without a scratch. When the war ended he was sent as Captain to the 5th Division Reception Camp.

It is unclear why he joined the Cheshire Regiment. His medal card only shows that and also his rank as Captain. The possibility is that he enlisted in Birmingham and was then commissioned into the Cheshire Regiment.

The 9th (Service) Battalion were formed in Chester on 13th September 1914 as part of K2 and came under orders of 58th Brigade, 19th (Western) Division. They moved to Salisbury Plain and by December 1914 were in billets in Basingstoke. They returned to Salisbury Plain in March 1915 before landing in France on 19th July 1915. They were concentrated near St. Omer. Their first action was at St. Pietre as part of the Battle of Loos (25th September to 8th October). They also fought at the Battle of the Somme taking part in the capture at La Boisselle and had also been involved in the attacks at High

Wood, the Battle of Pozieres, the Ancre Heights, the Ancre. In 1917 they were in action in the Battle of Messines and the Third Battle of Ypres. On 7th February 1918 they transferred to the 56th Brigade in the same Division. During 1918 they were involved in most of the battles. They fought against the German Spring Offensive in March 1918 in the Battle of St. Quentin and the Battle of Bapaume and then the Battle of Lys around Messines in April and the Battle of Ballieul and the Battle of Kemel Ridge. They were also involved in the final battles of the war from August to November. These included the Battle of the Aisne, and in the Final Advance into Picardy they were involved in the Battle of the Selle, the Battle of the Sambre and the Passage of the Grand Honelle.

Looking at the list of battles he was involved in it is fairly staggering that he came through without a single injury especially given the fact that the death rate among junior officers was extremely high.

He was killed on *30th March 1920* whilst riding a motorcycle and sidecar which was in collision with a tram on the corner of Russell Road and Edgbaston Road. This raises the question as to why Ashfield felt it necessary to put his name on their war memorial. This is pure speculation but at the inquest the tram conductor mentioned his terrific speed before the collision. I wonder whether he ever came to terms with the fact that he had seen so many of his friends and fellow soldiers killed and maimed and yet he emerged from the war without a scratch!

And so we come to the last. Claude Johnson is buried in a family grave in Brandwood End Cemetery.

52. Captain Claude Johnson – Royal Army Medical Corps. He was the second son of Dr C.J.B. Johnson of Kings Heath. He joined *Ashfield Cricket Club* in 1902 on leaving Camp Hill Grammar School. He also played for Birmingham University and for the 'Nondescripts', a well-known Wednesday team. He was a keen, enthusiastic, energetic cricketer, a good bat, a very active fielder, and bowled a googly type ball. His greatest work for the Club was undoubtedly the substantial support that he gave to the projected  improvements in the playing area and pavilion accommodation in the years 1913 and 1914. He was also a prominent member of *Moor Green Football Club* as was his brother Stanfield. He went to Birmingham University to study medicine where he excelled, passing his medicine and surgery examinations at only 21 and was the youngest medical graduate of the University when he qualified in 1908. Soon after graduating he became Resident Medical Officer at the General Hospital, Birmingham and was the Assistant Obstetrics at the Queens. He was also non-resident House Surgeon at Moseley Hall Convalescent Hospital for Children.

He was called up when war broke out as he was on the Army Medical Special Reserve and went to France with the British Expeditionary Force on 21st August 1914. He was immediately caught up with fighting following the Battle of Mons, 23rd-24th August and the subsequent retreat, working in a casualty clearing station. On the night of the 25th August 1914 he was with the 4th (Guards) Brigade as they fought the Germans in the streets of the town of Landrecies holding off the superior forces long enough to enable the BEF to retreat and when their task was completed they too retreated in good order. Following this action he was promoted to Captain and was posted to sanitary duty due to his experience in Public Health. He was then sent to India where he served until the end of the war. He was based at Jhelum where he was in charge of the health of the troops in the area. Whilst there he had a severe attack of dysentery which weakened his health considerably.

When he returned to England he resumed his medical practice in Kings Heath, living at Rockmount. In May 1919 he married Elin Liebbrandt, who had served as a nurse in the War. They married at St. Michaels, Handsworth, with his brother-in-law conducting the service. He continued to play cricket and was captain of Moseley Ashfield for the 1919 season helping to re-establish the club after the losses and disruption of the War. He had high hopes for Ashfield at the start of the 1920 season and had also agreed to play for the Wednesday section of Kings Heath Cricket Club. Unfortunately he had played his last innings. With his health weakened by war he succumbed to a bout of pneumonia and died aged 36 on *15th May 1920*.

The War had a profound effect on all four clubs. At the Annual General Meeting held at Moseley Rugby Club in October 1919 the Chairman, J.F. Byrne, announced that at least 11 past members of the club had been killed (the memorial has 16) with a further 70 wounded. The loss of revenue for the Club meant that it was in a precarious financial position and he made an appeal to the members of the club as well as the residents of Moseley for a £1,000 to '... place the club on a sound financial basis.' He went on to point out to the residents of

Unveiling the Memorial at Moseley Rugby Club.

Moseley the high regard in which the 'Reds and Blacks' were held across the rugby playing world and that without Moseley Rugby Club '... this delightfully situated spot would have, long ago, been built upon, probably with jerry-built houses!' on 19th October 1921 a memorial to the 16 men from the club who lost their lives, was unveiled at the Reddings.

Moseley Golf Club was less affected and was able to buy the freehold of their course in 1919. They too erected a plaque to the fallen in their clubhouse.

The Moseley Rugby Club Memorial which is now once more at the club.

The Moseley Golf Club Memorial.

The close ties between Ashfield Cricket Club and Moor Green Football Club, with Mr Bache being president of both meant that they had a joint memorial. The *Moseley and Kings Heath Journal* had paid tribute to Ashfield in an article in March 1919 entitled 'The Fighting Ashfields'. In this article they mentioned the fact that 90 per cent of the members had volunteered for service in 1914 and had served in virtually every theatre of the war with a member being present at the Battle of Mons in 1914 and another entering Mons again on Armistice Day, 11th November 1918. Their joint memorial was unveiled by Mr W.B. Bache on 23rd April 1921.

The Ashfield Cricket Club and Moor Green Football Club Memorial.

We Will Remember Them

	Name	Regiment	Death	Team
1	Private George Pearce	3rd Battalion Worcestershire Regiment	23/08/1914	Moseley Rugby Club
2	Lieutenant Vernon James Austin	22nd Battery 34th Brigade Royal Field Artillery	26/01/1915	Moseley Rugby Club
3	2nd Lieutenant Gilbert Rowland Venables	3rd Battalion King's Shropshire Light Infantry	07/03/1915	Moseley Rugby Club
4	Lieutenant Frederick Bonham Burr	3rd Battalion Worcestershire Regiment	12/03/1915	Ashfield Cricket Club
5	Captain John Francis	1st /5th Battalion Royal Warwickshire	02/06/1915	Moseley Rugby Club
6	Captain Norman Kingsley Street	9th Battalion Worcestershire Regiment	10/08/1915	Moseley Rugby Club
7	Lance Corporal Edward Thomas Blackham	Queen's Own Worcestershire Hussars (Worcester Yeomanry)	28/08/1915	Ashfield Cricket Club
8	2nd Lieutenant George Walter Field	10th Battalion Gloucestershire Regiment	25/09/1915	Moor Green Football Club
9	Lance Corporal Charles Leonard Ovens	2nd Battalion Oxford and Bucks Light Infantry	25/09/1915	Moseley Rugby Club
10	2nd Lieutenant Douglas Howard Wilson Greenway	13th Battalion Worcestershire Regiment	17/10/1915	Moseley Golf Club
11	Staff Quartermaster Sergeant Maurice William Hobson	Queen's Own Worcestershire Hussars (Worcester Yeomanry)	23/04/1916	Ashfield Cricket Club

	Name	Regiment	Death	Team
12	2nd Lieutenant Philip Leslie Patterson	1st Battalion North Staffordshire Regiment	04/06/1916	Moseley Rugby Club
13	2nd Lieutenant John Balkwill	6th Battalion Royal Warwickshire Regiment	01/07/1916	Ashfield Cricket Club
14	2nd Lieutenant Frank Aldridge Fawcett	1st/5th Battalion South Staffordshire Regiment	01/07/1916	Ashfield Cricket Club
15	Lieutenant Harold Egbert Foizey	18th Battalion West Yorkshire Regiment (Prince of Wales's Own)	01/07/1916	Ashfield Cricket Club
16	2nd Lieutenant William Henry Furse	21st (Tyneside Scottish) Battalion Northumberland Fusiliers	01/07/1916	Ashfield Cricket Club
17	2nd Lieutenant William Worthington Sanby	20th (Tyneside Scottish) Battalion Northumberland Fusiliers	01/07/1916	Moor Green Football Club
18	Private George Albert Davis	2nd Battalion (Duke of Edinburgh's) Wiltshire Regiment	08/07/1916	Moor Green Football Club
19	Captain George Pendrell Blake	10th Battalion Royal Welsh Fusiliers	20/07/1916	Moseley Golf Club
20	Corporal Ernest Clifford Hill	14th Battalion Royal Warwickshire Regiment	23/07/1916	Ashfield Cricket Club
21	Private William Ernest Stubbs	14th Battalion Royal Warwickshire Regiment	23/07/1916	Moor Green Football Club
22	Private John Edward Chilton Price	14th Battalion Royal Warwickshire Regiment	23/07/1916	Moor Green Football Club
23	Private George Joseph Griffiths	15th Battalion Royal Warwickshire Regiment	23/07/1916	Moor Green Football Club
24	2nd Lieutenant Rowland Evan Basil Rowlands	16th Battalion (3rd Birmingham Pals) Royal Warwickshire Regiment	27/07/1916	Moor Green Football Club
25	Captain William Herbert Hedges	1st (North Midland) Field Company, Royal Engineers	22/08/1916	Moseley Rugby Club
26	Private Phillip Reeves Vaughton	1st/14th Battalion London Scottish Regiment	02/09/1916	Moseley Rugby Club

	Name	Regiment	Death	Team
27	Lance Corporal Charles Chester Illingworth	15th Battalion (2nd Birmingham Pals) Royal Warwickshire Regiment	03/09/1916	Moor Green Football Club
28	Private William Anthony Machin	16th Battalion Middlesex Regiment	24/11/1916	Moor Green Football Club
29	Captain James Neilson Greenlees Stafford	6th Battalion Royal Warwickshire Regiment	16/04/1917	Moseley Rugby Club
30	Lieutenant Alistair MacNiven	7th Battalion Cameron Highlanders	01/05/1917	Moor Green Football Club
31	Captain John Chamberlain Military Cross	14th Battalion Welsh Regiment	14/05/1917	Moseley Rugby Club
32	Private Edward O'Brien	2nd London Sanitary Company	14/08/1917	Ashfield Cricket Club
33	Lieutenant (Edmund) Kenneth Wallace Brown	3rd/5th Battalion Royal Warwickshire Regiment	24/08/1917	Moseley Rugby Club
34	Lieutenant George Elliot Austin	6th Battalion Royal Warwickshire Regiment	27/08/1917	Ashfield Cricket Club
35	Lieutenant Hugh Randolph Ryan-Bell	1st/8th Battalion Worcestershire Regiment	29/08/1917	Ashfield Cricket Club
36	2nd Lieutenant Harry Raymond Rawlinson	1st/8th Battalion Machine Gun Corps (Infantry)	26/09/1917	Moor Green Football Club
37	Private Frederic Howard Inns	2nd Battalion Honourable Artillery Company	09/10/1917	Ashfield Cricket Club
38	Lieutenant William James Pearce	2nd/5th Battalion Gloucestershire Regiment	02/12/1917	Moseley Rugby Club
39	Captain Roland Bevington Gibbins	2nd/8th Battalion Royal Warwickshire Regiment	03/12/1917	Moseley Rugby Club
40	Captain Leysters Llewellyn Greener Military Cross	2nd/6th Battalion Royal Warwickshire Regiment	05/12/1918	Moseley Rugby Club
41	2nd Lieutenant Gerald Edward Drake	10th Battalion Worcestershire Regiment	26/01/1918	Moseley Golf Club

	Name	Regiment	Death	Team
42	Private Frederick Arthur Woodcock	14th Battalion (1st Birmingham Pals) Royal Warwickshire Regiment	03/02/1918	Moor Green Football Club
43	Captain Walter Reynolds Mansell	5th Battalion South Staffordshire Regiment	16/04/1918	Moseley Rugby Club
44	Gunner Wilfred Leslie Hales	280th Siege Battery Royal Garrison Artillery	24/04/1918	Moor Green Football Club
45	Private Herbert Leslie Tomlinson	"C" Battery 58th Brigade Royal Field Artillery	22/05/1918	Moor Green Football Club
46	Captain Charles Leslie Young	Royal Air Force	30/05/1918	Moor Green Football Club
47	Private Alfred Blackham	Royal Army Medical Corps	21/06/1918	Moor Green Football Club
48	Captain Charles Walter Hughes	14th Battalion (1st Birmingham Pals) Royal Warwickshire	01/10/1918	Moseley Golf Club
49	2nd Lieutenant Stanley Phillips Fryer	30th Brigade Royal Field Artillery	27/10/1918	Moor Green Football Club
50	Captain Hugh Lancelot Evers Military Cross and Bar	2nd/8th Battalion Worcestershire Regiment	01/11/1918	Moseley Rugby Club
51	Captain Sydney Graham Halsey	9th Battalion Cheshire Regiment	30/03/1920	Ashfield Cricket Club
52	Captain Claude Johnson	Royal Army Medical Corps	15/05/1920	Ashfield Cricket Club

By the Same Author

Cheer Boys It's Hartlebury!

The Story of Hartlebury Voluntary Aid
Detachment Hospital in World War I

ISBN: 978-1-85858-570-3   RRP: £14.95